Holger Nauroth

THE LUFTWAFFE

FROM THE NORTH CAPE TO TOBRUK 1939-1945 •

An Illustrated History

Translated from the German by Don Cox

SCHIFFER MILITARY HISTORY
West Chester, PA

Dust jacket artwork by Steve Ferguson, Colorado Springs, Colorado.

On the Dust Jacket:

Front: The plane overhead is a **Messerschmitt Me-262** and was flown by the elite pilots of *Kommando Nowotny* in the fall of 1944. Illustrated is ship #8 flown by the Kommando's famous namesake, Major Walter Nowotny, the first pilot to claim 250 victories. A recipient of the highest service citation, Nowotny was killed in #8 by a swarm of Eighth AF P-51s who ambushed the commander when he tried to land after a combat sortie on November 8, 1944 – a fate shared by so many of the great "experten" of the late war era,.

The **Messerschmitt Bf 109 F-2** flown by (then) Hauptmann Werner Molders is shown below. The aircraft shown is the one Molders used in late 1940 when the pilot assumed command of JG 51 and scored his 50th victory over the English Channel. Molders was the principal innovator of the modern tactics adopted by Fighter Command and after a year of combat over the western front, became the General of Fighters for the Luftwaffe extant. Molders was also the first German pilot to claim 100 aerial victories, and subsequently the first to receive the highest service award, the Knight's Cross garnished with oak leaves, crossed swords and diamonds. He was killed in an He 111 on November 22, 1941 en route to Germany.

Back: Above is a nightfighter variant of the **Junkers Ju 88 C-6c** bomber, flown by Prussian nobleman and leading "night ace" of 1943, Major Prince zu Sayn-Wittgenstein. At the time of his death, the "prince of the nightfighters" had scored the majority of his 83 night kills in the big radar equipped fighter, but Wittgenstein was lost in combat in January of 1944 before he could receive the diamond garnish for his Knight's Cross with oak leaves and swords. His score was eventually surpassed by two other nightfighter pilots later in the war. At the time of his death, the major was Kommodore of NJG 2, the "nachtgruppe" which ended the war with the highest night victory score in the Luftwaffe.

Below is a **Junkers Ju 87 G-2**, one of many "STUKA"s flown by Oberleutnant Hans-Ulrich Rudel. The aircraft illustrated is Rudel's "tank killer" armed with two under-wing 37mm cannon, which he flew while Kommodore of the famous *Immelmann Stukagruppe* in late 1944. Rudel was accredited with a score of well over 2500 tanks destroyed in his three continuous years of flight duty on the Russian front. The colonel was the highest decorated flyer in the Luftwaffe, receiving the oak leaves, swords and diamonds garnish for his one-of-a-kind gold Knight's Cross. Rudel died in 1982.

Translated from the German by Don Cox.

Library of Congress Catalog Number: 91-61441.

Printed in the United States of America.
ISBN: 0-88740-361-1

This title was originally published under the title,
Die Deutsche Luftwaffe vom Nordkap bis Tobruk 1939-1945,
by Podzun-Pallas Verlag, Friedberg.

We are interested in hearing from authors with book ideas on related topics. We are also looking for good photographs in the military history area. We will copy your photos and credit you should your materials be used in a future Schiffer project.

Published by Schiffer Publishing, Ltd.
1469 Morstein Road
West Chester, Pennsylvania 19380
Please write for a free catalog.
This book may be purchased from the publisher.
Please include $2.00 postage.
Try your bookstore first.

CONTENTS

INTRODUCTION

This book is intended to be neither a technically nor chronologically precise reference work. Rather, its aim is to portray the relationship between man and weapon through the use of words and, especially, photographs. It shows men who willingly performed their duty out of a strong belief in the necessity of their mission, or considered it a patriotic obligation given their perspective and the situation during that time. There have already been volumes written about how the idealistic values of entire generations were misused for ambiguous, and later criminal goals. It should not be, and is not, the purpose of this photojournal to show otherwise.

Organized in seven chapters according to the campaigns fought both consecutively and concurrently, this work attempts to fully retrace the Luftwaffe's transformation, especially that experienced by its people under the changing conditions.

For those who were directly involved, the photograph is a natural way to graphically bring back long-forgotten memories; for those who didn't experience that harsh period of time, the photograph provides a better and more informative understanding. These feelings are enhanced knowing that none of the photos in this collection were taken from the material recorded by the official propaganda photographers of the time. Instead, the vast majority of the material in this book comes from private sources, hidden for years in dusty shoeboxes. Luftwaffe operations during the Second World War are portrayed in approximately 500 photos, most of them published here for the first time. Within these pages you'll not only find the famous heroes, but also those everyday pilots, ground crew, and others upon whose faces were etched the strain of those operations. The civilian population and their suffering should not be excluded, either.

The focus of this collection is on the Jagdwaffe, the fighter arm of the Luftwaffe. This branch in particular suffered drastic changes through the course of the war. Highly praised and initially heaped with awards and decorations, their pilots gradually sank into disfavor in the eyes of the narrow-minded and incapable leadership -especially Hitler's. They became the scapegoats for all the mistakes and negligence of those in the highest leadership positions, who continued on with their policies in total ignorance of reality.

In preparing the book, the author has made extensive use of foreign sources. A large number of photos in this book were gleaned from the Imperial War Museum in London and the Department of Defense in Washington. To complete the work, French sources were also used.

At this point I would like to thank all those who have supported my efforts with photos, documents, and information. I would especially like to express my gratitude to the following persons and institutions who have made such a contribution to the success of this volume. They are Messrs. Boos, Eickhoff, Ernst, Galland, Gärtner, Geisinger, Happel, Heinrich, Holz, Kempf, Leykauf, Lorant, Nacke, Neumann, Prets, Riedel, Robel, Schob, Scholl, Schröder, Stuka, Trautloft, and Wahl, as well as the Department of the Air Force, USA, Office of Public Affairs, USA, the Imperial War Museum, London, the RAF, and the USAF. Last but not least, I would also like to thank my wife Ute, who not only mustered up the necessary patience, but also energetically supported me with her cooperation.

A SEASON OF EASY VICTORIES

The little-used aircraft of the Luftwaffe didn't fill much more than a propaganda role during the march into the Rhineland, the occupation of the Sudetenland, and the annexation of Austria. This was not to be the case in Spain. The flying units of the Legion Condor played a decisive role in the victories that the Spanish Nationalist units scored over their opponents. They showed the enormous possibilities of the tactical use of air power in combined ground-air operations. For the first time the strategic employment of air power was also effectively demonstrated to its fullest. As the whole world watched, the fighters, Stukas, and other combat aircraft faced their first big trial by fire. While the fighters successfully disrupted enemy air operations or carried out escort duty for their own bombers, the Stukas and attack aircraft supported Franco's troops in their operations as flying artillery - with great success.

During the Polish campaign, which began almost exactly one year after the Spanish Civil War ended, the tried and true methods used so successfully in Spain would be employed again.

The campaigns to secure the northwest flanks against Belgium and Holland posed no problems for the Luftwaffe. The technical, organizational, and personnel superiority of the Luftwaffe's flying units was too great. And then, in addition to all that, there was the outstanding training given to the German soldier.

The combination of air and ground operations came as a complete surprise to the opponents of Germany during these "Blitzkrieg" campaigns. The freedom of individual service branches, such as the Luftlandetruppen (airborne assault troops), the various air commands within the Luftwaffe, or the Panzertruppen (armored units) of the Heer was totally new to the western as well as the eastern enemies, who had nothing with which to counter their tactics. During the continuing course of the war, the German leadership unfortunately demonstrated that it had learned nothing from the mistakes of its enemies; they even began to work against their own tried and true principles and gradually lost control of the fate of Germany.

6

In 1937 final delivery of these Bf 109 C-2s was made to JG 26; these aircraft represented the most powerful and modern air force in the world. Barely three years after regaining military sovereignty, Germany had at its disposal a magnificent weapon.

On the eve of September 1st, these Hs 126 tactical reconnaissance aircraft stand ready near the Polish border, camouflaged by trees. The next morning, the most terrible conflict of all time would begin.

At daybreak on the 1st of September, 1939, shortly after 4:00am, the first and second Gruppen of StG 2, "Immelmann", launched their aircraft from several different airfields in Germany against targets in Poland - the Stukas have attacked.

The Ju 87 Stuka had been planned and built as a dive bomber. It was the decisive factor in the initial successes of the Wehrmacht. The aircraft dove vertically at the target as this photograph so impressively demonstrates.

Takeoff on an operational sortie. With engine running, a Bf 109 waits for clearance to take off.

The aircraft from I/JG 1 take off in Rotten (pairs) on a bomber escort mission.

Once airborne the landing gear struts of the Messerschmitt fighter retract one after another.

A Polish grass landing strip has been overrun by rapidly advancing German troops; in the foreground is a burned out Polish PZL 11 fighter, in the background can be seen the remains of a bomber.

After returning from a mission, this Bf 109 is readied for another sortie. Apparently, there was something wrong with the radio since the technician in the foreground has removed the access cover, behind which the radio is located.

From time to time the Radom air base hosted practically everything in the German Luftwaffe inventory: a large number of Ju 87s, as well as Hs 123s, Ju 52s, Fi 156s, and Bf 110s.

The headquarters flight of IV/JG 132 stands in the sun on a grass landing strip in Poland. The triangular markings on the Bf 109 E-1 in the foreground indicate that it is the aircraft of the Gruppe commander. Behind it is the Gruppe adjutant's aircraft.

Hitler visiting the victorious pilots in Poland. The campaign is finished. At the far left beneath the upraised arm is a combat pilot who would become famous as a fighter: Oberleutnant Adolf Galland.

The Polish air force, poorly equipped and even more poorly led, would be for the most part destroyed on the ground. The Poles had succeeded in moving some of their bombers and fighters away from the airfields. It was at these dispersed areas, however, that they would soon become victims of the superior German fighters or Bf 110 Zerstörer (Destroyers) - despite the Poles' valiant courage.

The PZL 11, the basic Polish fighter, was hopelessly outclassed; in spite of the courage demonstrated by the Polish fighter pilots it was a completely outdated design.

The PZL 37 Los B was, on the other hand, a significantly more modern medium bomber. It saw relatively little action, however.

The PZL 23 was utilized as a close air support aircraft and enjoyed successes against German army units. However, there were too few of these aircraft available to the Poles.

A Bf 109 E-1 of II/JG 132 at an airfield in Poland.

Lt. Seiler of I/JG 54 making last minute adjustments before takeoff.

Big cleaning day for the newly-formed II/JG 26 on the northwestern German border - November 1939.

The symbol of JG 26 was an "S", which stood for the last name of Albert Leo Schlageter, a resistance fighter shot by the French during their occupation of the Ruhr. The raven was the sign of 5 Staffel. The Bf 109 has been well camouflaged through the use of hay and tarpaulins.

There was a great rush to equip the fighter units with the new Messerschmitt fighter. Given the hectic pace at which the conversion took place, it was natural that there would be losses of both material and personnel.

II Gruppe of JG 77 assumed the responsibilities of fighter protection with their Bf 109 E-4 aircraft. Even at this airfield, wooden boards had to be laid down in the extremely soft earth of the dispersal areas so that the fighters could remain operationally ready.

Heinrich Ehrler, having transferred from an anti-aircraft unit to train as a fighter pilot in 1940, arrived in Norway in 1941. Following his 112th aerial victory on August 2nd, 1943, he was awarded the Oak Leaves to the Knight's Cross for his outstanding performance.

Messerschmitt Bf 110C aircraft set out against the enemy from their new bases in Denmark and Norway. The kill markings on the rudder indicate that the crew of these two Zerstörer have been successful before.

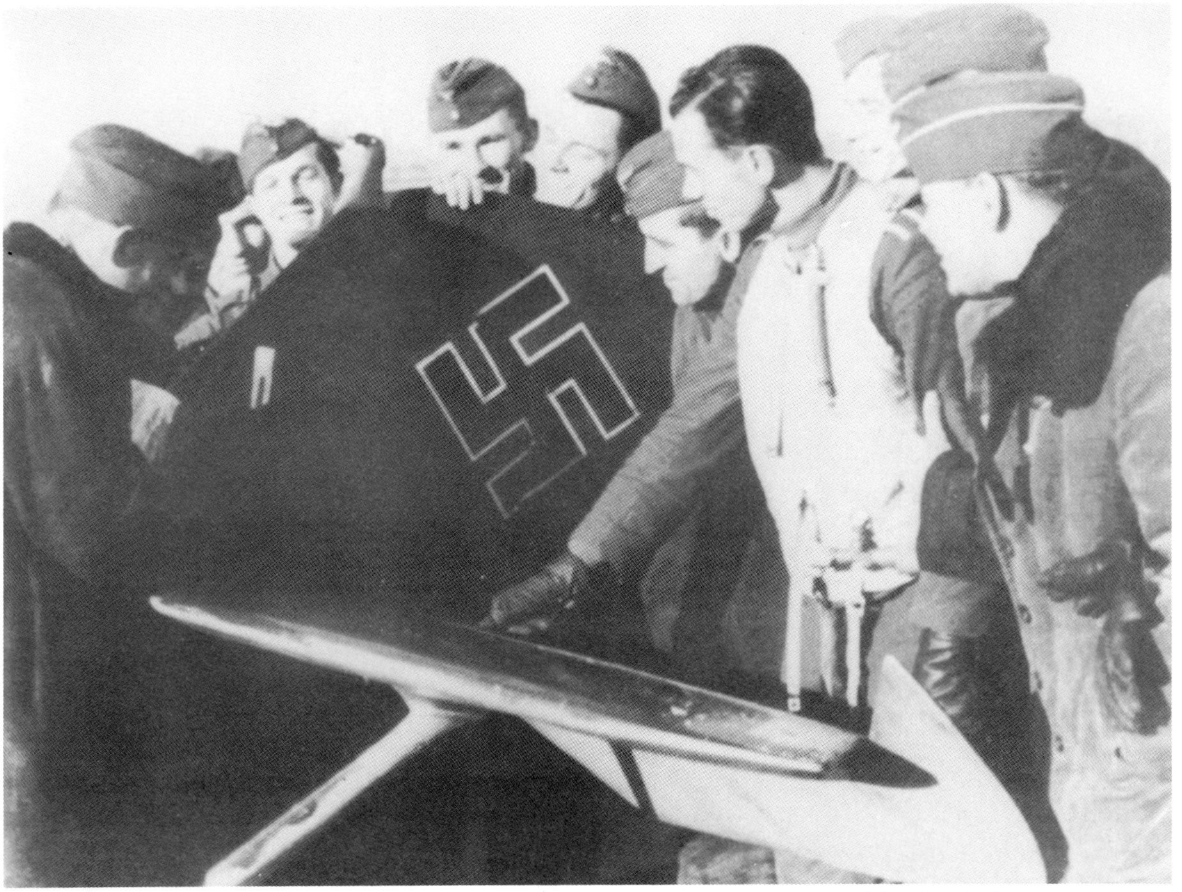

On September 4th, 1939, Uffz. Held became the first German pilot to shoot down a British bomber in the Second World War. Here he proudly observes a ground crewman painting the kill marking on the rudder of his Bf 109.

More successes soon follow. The thrill of victory is still quite strong, for the nightmare of constant day-to-day combat has not yet begun.

A Bf 109 E-3 returns from a patrol, coming in for a landing on the snow-covered airfield of JG 77's II Gruppe.

At rest in the noontime winter sun.

The Bf 109 E-1 had a very good rate of climb. This Gruppe has been tasked with bomber escort duty.

This time it's the Staffeln of KG 2 with their Do 17Z aircraft that have been brought safely to their targets by the fighters.

The target is a stretch of railway in western Poland. Just as the bombers reach the target - a depot for the Polish Army - a train carrying supplies arrives. Bombs away!

The seventh car from the end has taken a hit from a bomb and is burning; above the train can be seen stacked goods, and to the left are bomb trenches.

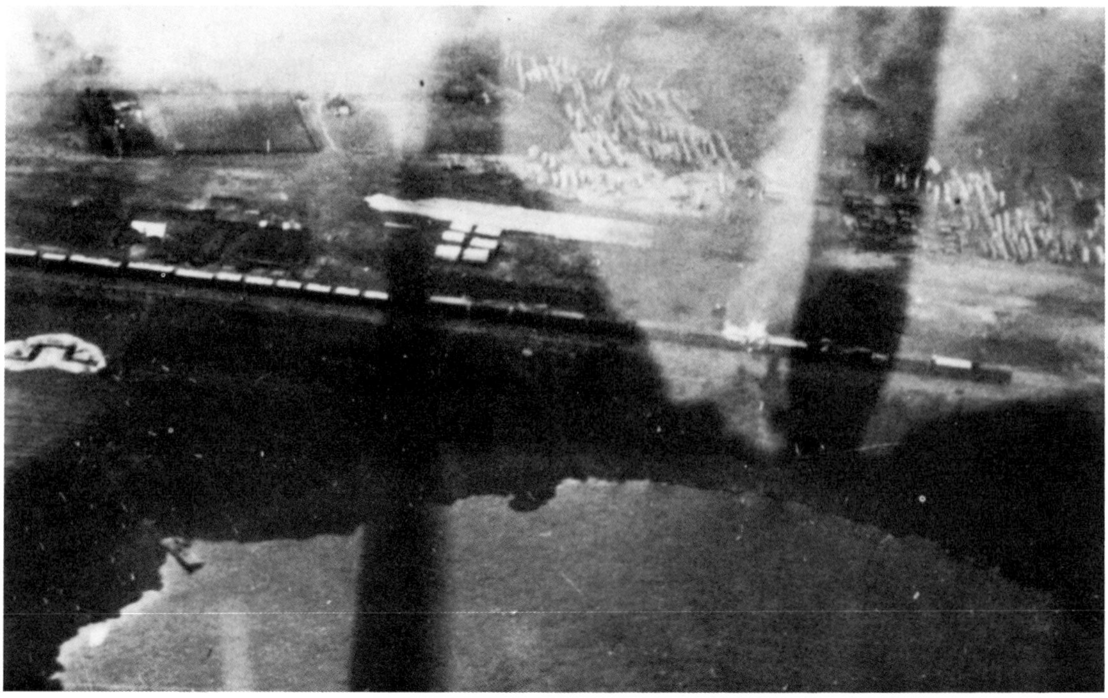

In the northern part of the Reich the Messerschmitt fighters of JG 77 take on the role of protection against enemy incursions.

Scramble! The alert Kette is already airborne.

English Wellington bombers approaching the German coast.

This photo shows the remains of the Wellington bombers, which were detected on the 18th of December, 1939 by a prototype of the first German radar system, "Freya", on Wangerooge, as the aircraft approached the German coast. The fighters of JG 1 were alerted and succeeded in shooting down 12 of the 24 English bombers, which by then had turned for home.

The great tragedy in the death of so many English airmen lay in the fact that the RAF - in spite of the existing state of war - was using completely inexperienced crews to carry out a navigational flight without bombs against the German port of Wilhelmshaven.

The war also reached into northern Europe. Shortly before the English were to occupy Norway, the combined naval, land, and air forces of Germany succeeded in reaching Norway, thereby securing the northern flank.

Under fire from machine guns and light artillery the first wave of German Zerstörer and bombers landed, being forced to do so because of their low fuel state. Numerous aircraft were damaged due to the poor conditions of the Norwegian airfields; in the foreground can be seen a Bf 110 of 2/ZG 76, and in the background an He 111 of KG 100, both of which were forced to land at Oslo-Fornebu.

A forward airfield has been quickly built in Norway using wooden planks, and the "Zerstörer" of I/ZG 76 are ready to take off. External fuel tanks have been added to increase the range.

The Luftwaffe played a particularly important role in the war over the ocean at the beginning of the Second World War. An He 115 floatplane flies a reconnaissance patrol off the Norwegian coast. This type also had the capability to drop torpedoes.

A Do 18D-2 of the 2nd Kü.Fl.Gr. 406 is ready for takeoff. The aircraft, which will be pushed into the water on rollers, still carries the pre-war camouflage pattern. This type was primarily used in the reconnaissance role.

Bombers return to base in tight formation as protection against the possible appearance of Polish fighters.

One of the successful combat pilots brings his plane in for a landing over the hangar of the airfield operations company.

The Hs 123 was a ground attack aircraft with dive bombing capabilities, used with success against Polish troops and supply columns.

With two 50kg bombs under each wing, a Kette of Hs 123 aircraft sets out against units of the Polish Army.

THE AIR WAR IN THE WEST

The "Sitzkrieg" had ended. Nearly eight months after England and France declared war on the German Reich the Wehrmacht attacked in the West. As outlined in the Schlieffen Plan, the German troops bypassed the Maginot Line, France's heavily fortified eastern line of defense. Like the sweeping cut of a sickle, the bunker positions of Belgium and Holland were circumvented and isolated from rear areas - from resupply - by quick thrusts from the Luftwaffe and tank units.

The Luftwaffe carried out the first strikes against the border fortifications and obstacles in Holland and, especially, in Belgium. Here, for the first time, a new branch of service proved itself - the paratroopers. While the Benelux nations has very little to offer in the way of air defense - Belgium still flew the outdated Gloster Gladiator biplane - it was expected that France would provide strong resistance. But the Armee de l'Air, equipped in part with modern aircraft, didn't fare any better than their colleagues in the Army, the tank corps. They were used as supplemental artillery in support of the Army, and their command and control was completely decentralized.

The Luftwaffe experienced the same successes in France as it did in Poland; during the first phase of the attack many French aircraft were destroyed on the ground, and the supplies, so necessary for the survival of the French Air Force, were either destroyed or rendered unusable. The situation was made even more favorable by virtue of the fact that the French Air Force, as opposed to their German enemy, conducted no type of planned aerial reconnaissance during the "Drole' de Guerre", or the Phoney War. The French government didn't take the war the least bit seriously, even though it was they, pressured by England, that had declared the war against Germany following the attack on Poland. The French High Command followed in step with its government and acted as if peace reigned supreme.

In the early morning hours on the 10th of May, 1940, German Do 17Z bombers overfly the French border.

The sun is on the rise. Looking out from the cockpit of a Do 17, the view leads across the gunsights of the MG 15 to the aircraft ahead.

Skillfully camouflaged, the fighters of II/JG 27 in the West await a new mission.

Visitors have arrived. Stukas now share the forward airfield with the fighters.

The "command post" of 6/JG 27 in the West; Lt. Wenzel, left, Lt. Neumann, right.

JG 27's second group carried the Berliner bear as its crest. The camouflage netting draped over the wings was designed to make the contours of the aircraft unrecognizable from the air.

JG 53, the "Pik-As" (Ace of Spades) Geschwader, also successfully took part in the Western Campaign.

A Potez 63 II, a light bomber of the Armee de l'Air, or the French Air Force, serves here as the background for a scrapbook photo of two French soldiers.

The landing gear was shot out from under this American-built Curtiss H 75 French fighter, causing a propeller to dig into the ground. The cockpit area was also heavily damaged.

The German fighters didn't get off so easy, either. This Bf 109 of III/JG 2 "Richthofen" is getting it's shot-up engine changed.

Even an open-air engine change isn't a headache for the "black men", as the mechanics in their black overalls were affectionately known. This is a scene at II/JG 51 taken on June 29th, 1940, in Desvres.

A 88mm flak gun mounted on a wheeled chassis advances past the Metz airfield, occupied by Zerstörer of II/ZG 76.

A 20mm flak gun takes up position at the edge of the airfield to protect it against low flying attackers.

"Zerstörer" aircraft of II/ZG 76, the "Haifisch" (shark) Gruppe, are fueled up. For a period of time during the French campaign this unit was scattered about various airfields.

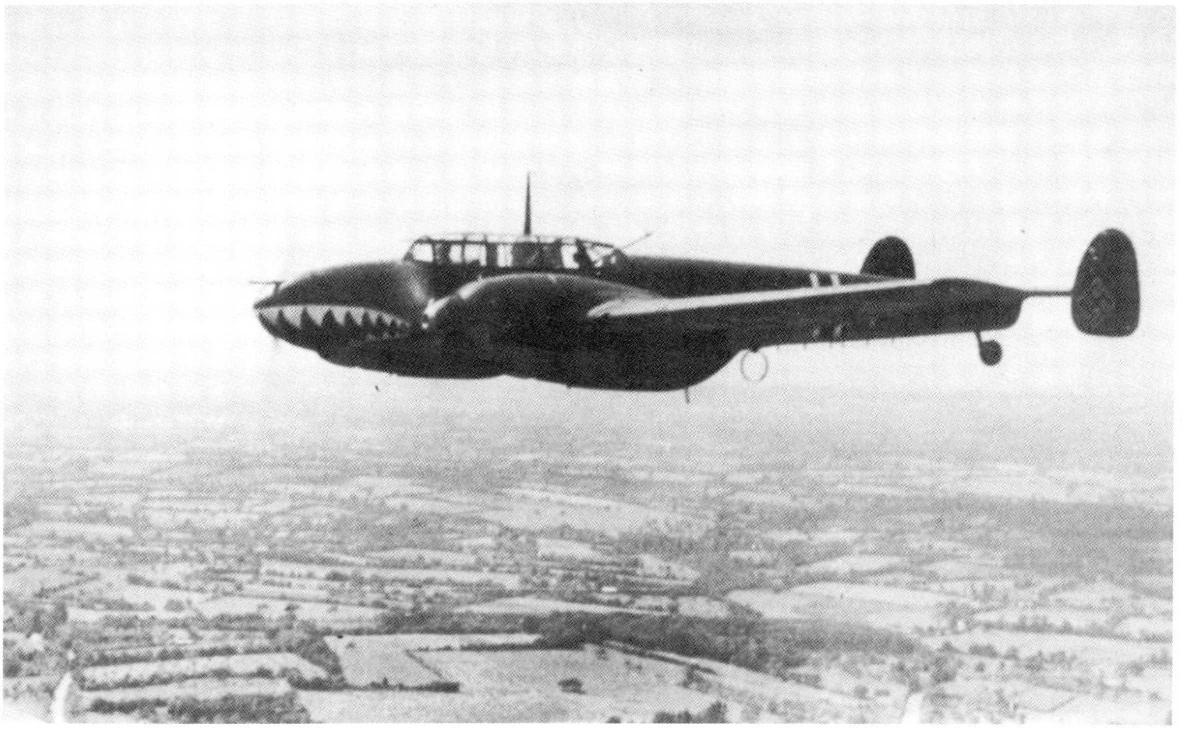

In northwestern France, in the Bretagne, Bf 110C aircraft carry out attacks against the fleeing French and English units.

This is the radio operator's view: the pilot wearing his soft helmet with its headphones and throat microphone connected to the radio via the cable running down the back of his neck; the gauges from left to right are: clock, fuel gauge, altimeter, speedometer, and ammunition gauge, which indicated number and type of rounds remaining in the machine gun.

This light French tank was a victim of a Zerstörer attack. The pilot is holding an unexploded 20mm shell that he found inside the tank.

There were also losses. After its mission this Bf 110 of II/ZG 76, with a shot out engine and hydraulic system, is pushed back into a camouflaged position.

Camouflage is still necessary in the first days of the war, as with this Do 17Z. It carries the paint scheme for night operations - both upper and lower surfaces are black.

This Do 17, well hidden beneath trees and netting, carries the more standard camouflage of the Luftwaffe. The underside of the wings and fuselage are light blue, the upper surfaces are a black-green/green splinter pattern.

A Bf 109 of JG 2 "Richthofen" is readied for a new mission. This "Emil" was photographed in France in August of 1940.

While the ground crewmen ready a Bf 109 E-3 for takeoff, the pilot puts on his oxygen mask.

Ground crewmen arm a Bf 110 C-7 of the III/ZG 26 "Horst Wessel." New, more difficult missions lie ahead. The French campaign was over with in a few short weeks and the air war over England had begun. This type was equipped with a fuselage mounted ETC rack to carry bombs. Touted as being one of the best, this long range fighter exhibited noticeable weaknesses during the dogfights against the more modern French Morane or Bloch fighters.

For now, however, the Luftwaffe basks in the glow of its shining victories. Nevertheless, many crewmen from KG 55, the "Greifen (griffin) Geschwader", seen here participating in the victory parade above Paris, died a senseless death a few months later over England.

Tourism à la Luftwaffe. Troops from an anti-aircraft unit take in the sights of Paris.

The remains of a Do 17, shot down by French fighters, are examined by Poilous.

This Bf 109, probably from JG 54, suffered a punctured radiator and was forced to make an emergency landing. This provided a photo opportunity for Uffz. Robel, a radio operator with the nearby II/ZG 76.

An Hs 126 being refuelled. This was the German standard tactical reconnaissance aircraft during the first years of the war.

Tactical reconnaissance aircraft - an important tool for the Heer's army leaders. Without these aircraft, the lightning quick successes of the troops would have hardly been considered possible.

Middle: The chocks are still in front of the wheels. The engine, however, is already running at full speed and soon this Hs 126 will take off to monitor French troop movements.

This impressive photo was taken near Paris from a Bf 110 flying as escort.

This Do 17P returned from a mission over enemy territory in a rather pitiful state. Aside from numerous machine gun hits in the cockpit area, the landing gear hydraulics have been shot out, forcing the pilot to make a belly landing.

These new Messerschmitt Bf 109 E-4 aircraft sit ready for operations at a forward airfield near the border.

On May 14th, 1940, the city and harbor of Rotterdam, which had been declared a fortress by the British, was attacked by 57 He-111 bombers. Because of surrender negotiations the formation was called back, but the order didn't reach the main group of bombers in time. This had devastating consequences for the downtown area.

Lt. Neumann, from II/JG 27, had to make an emergency landing near Brussels on May 21st 1940 around 8:35pm due to anti-aircraft fire damaging his aircraft's compressor.

THE GREAT CHALLENGE - BATTLE FOR THE SKIES OF ENGLAND

The Battle of Britain demonstrated that even the mighty German Luftwaffe had limits to its performance abilities. The goal of driving the British enemy from the skies and thereby laying the foundation for an invasion was never reached. Just as little success was achieved with the continuous bombardment of civilians in an attempt to demoralize them and break their will to resist. Certainly the main reason for the operation's failure was the constantly changing focus of the operation, directed by Hitler. Before a phase could be carried through to its conclusion, a new attack emphasis was created. The Luftwaffe, for example, was on the verge of obliterating the English fighter defense through constant attacks on airfields and supply depots in southern England when Hitler changed the focus of the campaign - to London. This provided an opportunity for the British fighters to recover from the devastating blow dealt them by the Luftwaffe and allowed the units, many of which were almost completely wiped out, to get back up to strength.

Another reason was certainly the fact that the Luftwaffe had reached the limits of its technical capabilities. Whereas the Bf 109 could not completely fulfill its role as an escort fighter due to its insufficient range, the Bf 110 quickly proved itself to be completely unsuited for the role for which it was designed - that of a long range fighter. It had neither the speed nor the maneuverability required of a fighter aircraft. Very soon it became necessary to provide fighter protection for the Bf 110. It was pretty much the same story with the Ju 87, used quite successfully in the Polish and French campaigns. The aircraft was far too unwieldy and too slow, and its insufficient defenses made it an easy prey for the enemy fighters. The Ju 87 was finally pulled from the Battle when the losses of men and material could no longer be justified. The Do 17 and He 111 bombers also possessed inadequate defensive armament and, additionally, suffered from a lack of sufficient armor protection. At the time of the Battle, their bomb load was not quite 1000kg which, given the number of aircraft used and the amount of sorties flown, was much too low to have any type of lasting effect.

In spite of their limited range and susceptibility to damage, it was the Bf 109 fighters that were able to hold their own in the air battles above England. In this context it should be noted that, at the height of the Battle of Britain, the German economy had only 30% of its resources converted to armaments manufacture - and the Luftwaffe wasn't anywhere near the top of the priorities list, unlike the situation with the English air forces.

Names like Lützow, Balthasar, Oesau, Wick, Galland, and Mölders were representative of the successful Jagdwaffe. They were the idols of that era, not because they had sought this status, but because the spirit of the times made them thus. But they, along with their fighter, bomber, Zerstörer, and Stuka brethren, soon lost the belief in a quick and easy victory. They had all joined the Luftwaffe to fulfill a dream as old as Man himself - the dream of flight! This dream of unfettered freedom became a reality for them, but too many paid for that dream with their health or their lives.

Left: A pilot from JG 26 prepares for takeoff in his Bf 109 E-4 while his crew chief helps him with his safety harness. The weapons crewman makes a last minute check of the weapons gauge on the instrument panel.

Center: In "Hanni 6000", or at an altitude of 6000m, fighters leave condensation trails behind them. They're flying towards a predetermined point that has been passed to them via radio.

That point is where the fighters join up with the bombers. These Do 17Z combat aircraft are still flying in close formation, awaiting their fighter escort.

Approximately 300km from the approaching German aircraft, these English fighter pilots wait for the order to scramble. They spend their nerve-wracking time waiting by reading or playing chess. In the next room can be seen a model of a Bf 109 on the table, used to better acquaint the pilots with its contours. The map behind the pilots shows the area of operations for this fighter group, the southeastern section of the British Isle.

The English fighters - such as this formation of Hurricanes taking off - were always warned in time where the enemy was approaching from and in which direction their target lay. This was made possible through the use of the early warning radar system, which masts can be seen in the background.

The distance to the target posed a greater problem for the escorting Messerschmitt fighters than did the English fighter defense. After takeoff, forming-up, flying to the target, and aerial combat there was often no fuel reserve left for the return flight. The last stop was often the beaches of northern France.

As was the case with these two fighters from JG 26, who were not able to make it back to a German airfield within the 90 minutes flight time allotted them.

Ofw. Meier tells his fellow pilot März and a mechanic about the mission he'd just flown - and his return flight as a glider pilot!

The mission briefing takes place in rather airy surroundings on the park grounds of the Château Monteclin near Villacoubley, a palace which served as the headquarters squadron for KG 55.

After the mission briefing it's off to the aircraft with parachute in hand.

50

Approaching the target - the approach altitude corresponded to Wetterlage 3 (weather condition 3), or 5000m. If the altitude were higher than this, the crew would be wearing oxygen masks.

These He 111 bombers from KG 55, the "Greifen-Geschwader", tighten their formation to provide better protection. The aircraft carried the coat of arms of the city of Giessen, a griffin (Greifen), directly behind the cockpit canopy.

In order to avoid being detected by the British radar, German bombers fly to their targets low over the Channel waters.

But the fighters of Fighter Command, such as these Spitfire MK 1a aircraft, were always well informed and lie in wait for the approaching German units.

A group of He 111s under attack. The right aircraft has already been hit and its right engine is burning. The tracer rounds can be made out quite easily.

The dogfight has fully erupted and the skies above England are covered with condensation trails caused by aircraft circling viciously around each other in the icy altitudes.

A Do 24T belonging to an air-sea rescue squadron stationed near Aalborg is readied for takeoff. Somewhere in the North Sea between England and Germany sits a German bomber crew in their liferaft, waiting for help after their bomber was shot up and forced to ditch.

A dramatic moment! As the pilots struggle to climb into the boarding hatch behind the cockpit, an English coastal patrol boat appears in the distance.

Fighter pilots after a mission.

. . . Uffz. Schiffer wears a look of elation following his third kill.

. . . Looking a bit worn out, Adolf Galland leaves his plane.

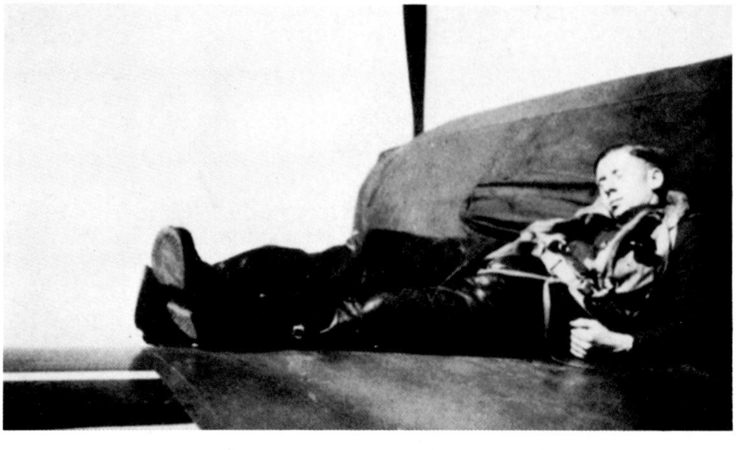

. . . Jupp Bigge enjoying a short nap in the sun.

Mechanics of I/JG 26 form up to check their tools.

A very important task was folding the parachute. The cabinet in the center of the picture holds a piece of test equipment for oxygen masks, which were worn by fighter pilots. To the right of the cabinet hang several life jackets. In the most serious situations, a pilot's life depended on these items working properly.

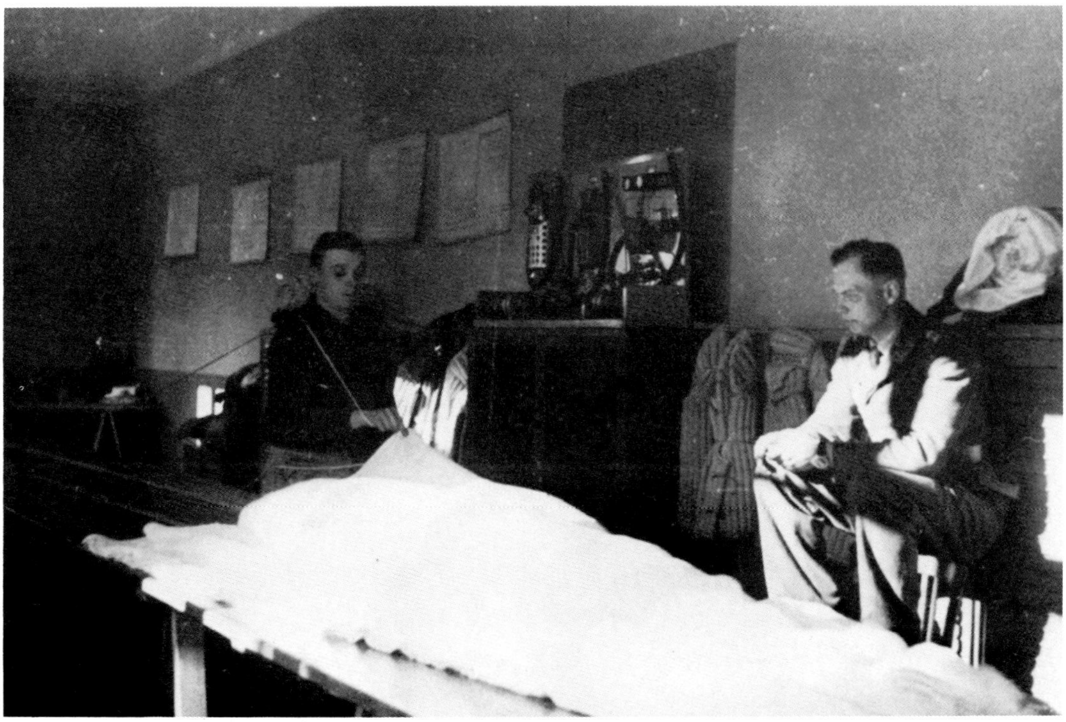

During the Battle of Britain the repair facilities at the airfield along the Channel were kept quite busy. At any given time almost all participating aircraft were represented at these facilities, such as here with an He 111, a Bf 109, and a Ju 88.

No repairs can help here, after a pilot of JG 2 accidentally drove his Bf 109 into the RDF shack.

JG 2's coat of arms has been applied beneath the cockpit of Uffz. Hippel's Bf 109. The "R" stands for Richthofen, whose name still carries a special meaning for pilots even today.

The typical hand gestures of a fighter pilot. The Leutnant of JG 26, like all fighter pilots, uses his hands to help him explain his latest aerial exploits.

Attempting to land after a check-out flight, the left landing gear of Uffz. Marquard's Bf 109 E-4 collapsed, forcing the pilot to crash land. The fuel tanks are being drained as a precautionary measure.

This aircraft of 5/JG 26 "Schlageter" had a new Daimler Benz DB 601 engine installed. Ogfr. Geisinger poses proudly in front of his installation work.

A Bf 110 of II/ZG 76 overflies the English southern coast. Its mission is to clear the way of enemy fighters for the approaching Stukas. A mission for which it became less and less suited.

The Ju 87, so successful in Poland and France, also did not perform as well as hoped for in the Battle of Britain. It suffered considerably due to its slow speed and poor armament and was finally pulled from operations.

The crew of a Bf 110 used for photo-reconnaissance duties maps out their flight route with the commander.

Next to the long range, the only plus for the Bf 110 was its powerful and concentrated firepower: 4 machine guns in the upper nose and 2 cannons mounted below.

This is most likely a maintenance flight, since the pilot isn't wearing a life jacket and other pieces of equipment are also missing. The pilot of a Bf 110 wore a seat parachute while the radio operator wore a back parachute.

German aircraft have been sighted - a Spitfire prepares to take off.

With the right engine already trailing smoke a new set of tracers, clearly visible, tears into the left wing. The photograph was taken from a Spitfire, which camera was linked to the guns. As soon as the guns began to fire the camera was automatically activated. Gun cameras were also used on the German side.

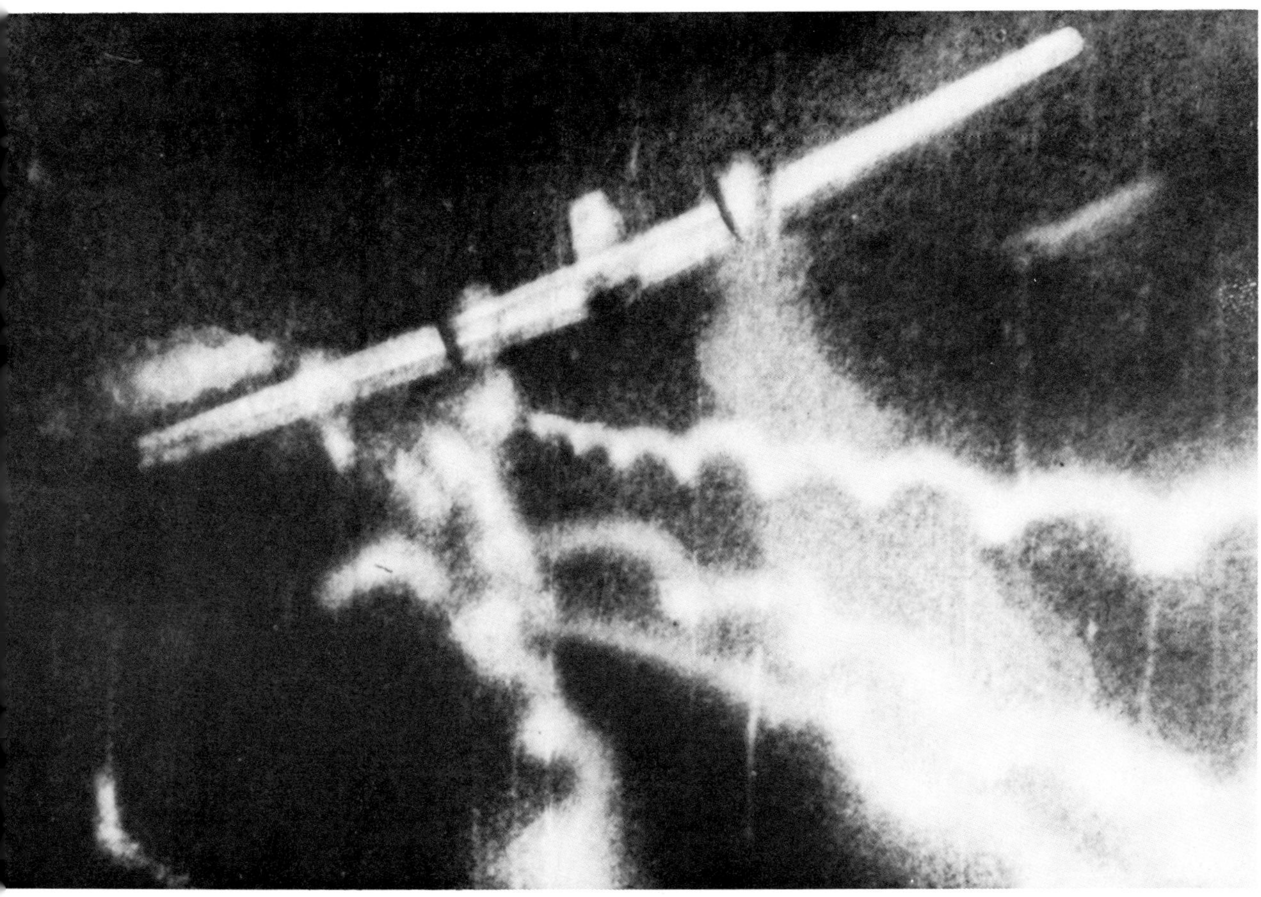

Nine new aircraft have arrived at the auxiliary airfield near Cognac on the southern canal front. That this is a replacement or training unit can be ascertained from the high aircraft numbers on the fuselage.

The same airfield also served as a training base to prepare young pilots for combat. They were made ready for front-line action through training provided by experienced pilots. This aircraft is the victim of a not-so-successful landing.

Forward airfields had to be built in order to provide the quickly advancing Heer with the vital air support it needed. This was the task of the Flughafenbetriebskompanien (airfield operations companies, or FBK). Here the FBK of LG 1 is laying out a new runway.

Foxholes are being dug next to the parking area of a Ju 88.

A revetment is being constructed here. This was a parking area designed to protect aircraft from shell fragments.

64 The famous Mickey Mouse being painted on the side of a replacement aircraft. This aircraft carries a red "1" instead of the arrow found on Galland's aircraft.

During the zenith of the Battle, Göring changed the leadership of the wings. Officers from the First World War were replaced by younger ones. The former commander of III Gruppe, Major Galland, assumed command of JG 26 at this time.

Galland's rudder on his Bf 109 already carried 84 kill markings.

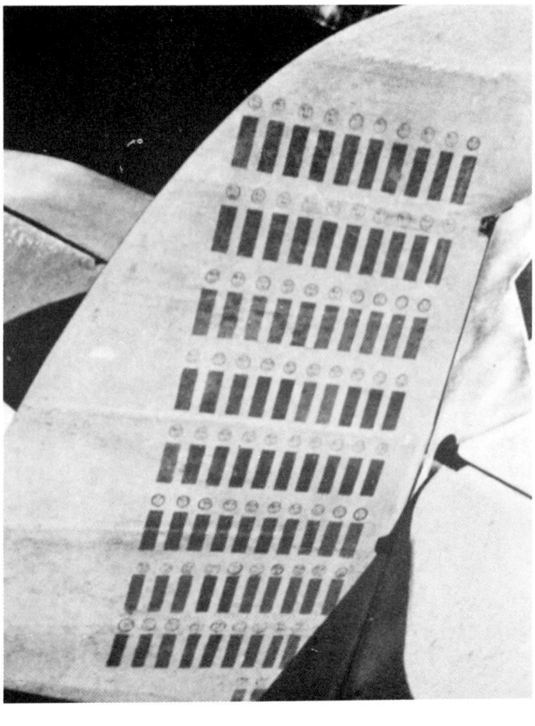

The new generation of Geschwader Kommodore (senior commanders), together with their Jagdführer, posing for the camera in Wissant; left to right: Major Galland JG 26, Major Lützow JG 3, Gen. Major Theo Osterkamp Jagdführer 2, Major Mölders JG 51, and Major von Maltzahn JG 53.

Hermann Göring, Reichsmarschall and Commander-in-Chief of the Luftwaffe, during a visit to the fighter Geschwader along the channel. The purpose of this visit was to make the fighter pilots aware of the drastically increasing losses being suffered by the bombers.

The fighters and Zerstörer did their best to fulfill their assigned task of protecting the bombers. The dead and missing of those days testified to their efforts. Funerals such as this one increased.

A Zerstörer crew prepares to take off, with Uffz. Paul Wenke as pilot and Gfr. Johann Heinrich as radioman.

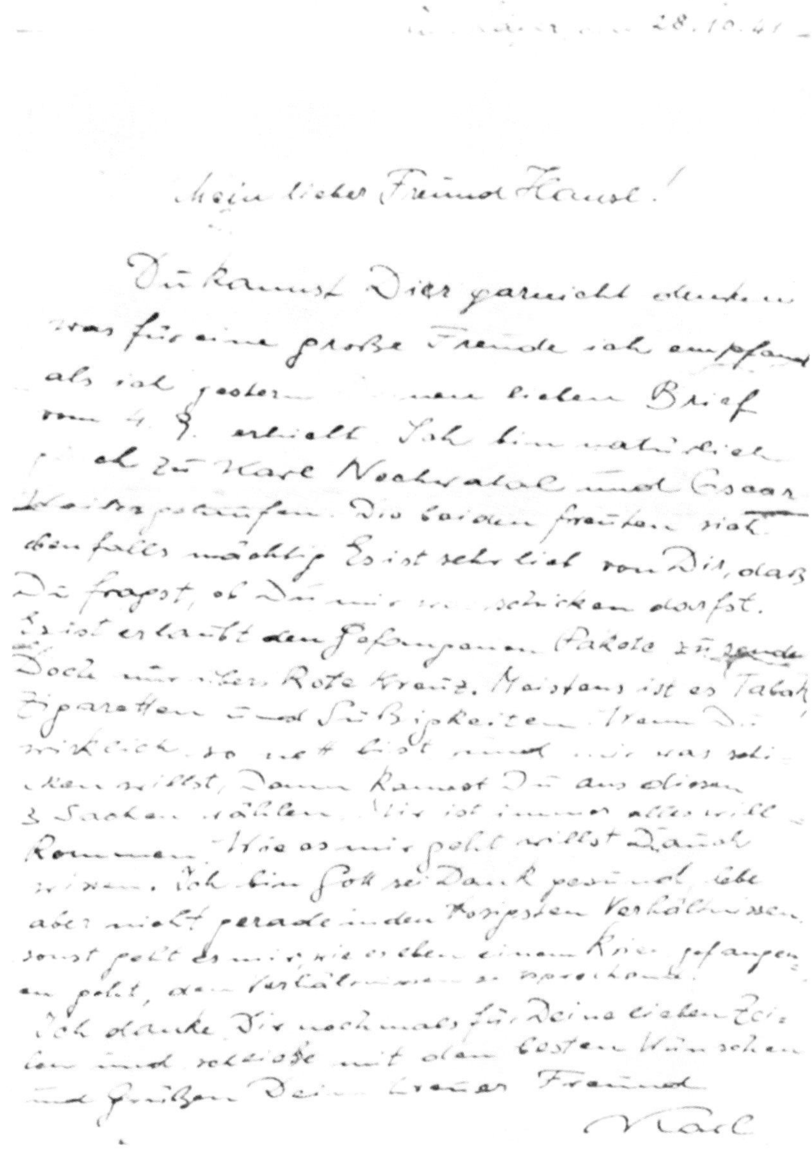

28.10.41

Mein lieber Freund Hansl!

Du kannst Dir garnicht denken was für eine große Freude ich empfand als ich gestern [illegible] lieben Brief vom 4.9. erhielt. Ich bin [illegible] Karl [illegible] und Oscar [illegible] Die beiden [illegible] Es ist sehr lieb von Dir, daß Du fragst, ob Du mir [illegible] schicken darfst. Es ist erlaubt den Gefangenen Pakete zu senden doch nur über Rote Kreuz. Meistens ist es Tabak, Zigaretten und Süßigkeiten. Wenn Du wirklich so nett bist und mir was schicken willst, dann kannst Du aus diesen 3 Sachen wählen. [illegible] Wie es mir geht willst Du auch wissen. Ich bin Gott sei Dank gesund, lebe aber nicht gerade in den [illegible] Verhältnissen, sonst geht es mir, wie es eben einem Kriegsgefangenen geht, den Verhältnissen entsprechend.

Ich danke Dir nochmals für Deine lieben Zeilen und schließe mit den besten Wünschen und Grüßen Dein [illegible] Freund

Karl

Many never returned from their missions. Those who were lucky were taken prisoner, such as the imprisoned writer of this letter, Uffz. Karl W. Stoff.

The receiver of the letter, which worked its way through International Red Cross channels, was the Gefreiter and radioman Johann Heinrich. He wears the normal ensemble, with helmet and throat microphone as well as the obligatory fur lined flying boots.

An interesting collection of photographs. This photo of Olt. Neumann of 6/JG 27 was taken at 1445 hours on August 18th 1940. Soon he would take off on a mission against the British radar site at Ventnore in southern England. The exposed film was later sent to his relatives, who, thinking the film hadn't been used, exposed it again.

This flight took place a few days prior to the 18th of August 1940; Olt. Neumann took the photograph. In the front, flying Red 10, is Uffz. Gromottka, Lt. Uebe in Red 2, and Fw. Krenz flying Red 4. This Schwarm was also flying together on the 18th, when Olt. Neumann took an anti-aircraft hit in the radiator and was forced to make an emergency landing on the Isle of Wight at 1530 hours.

An English press photographer took the next photo of Olt. Neumann as he departed Victoria Station under guard to for a long tenure as a prisoner of war.

The final entry in Olt. Neumann's log book was written in by his commander: "Failed to return from combat mission."

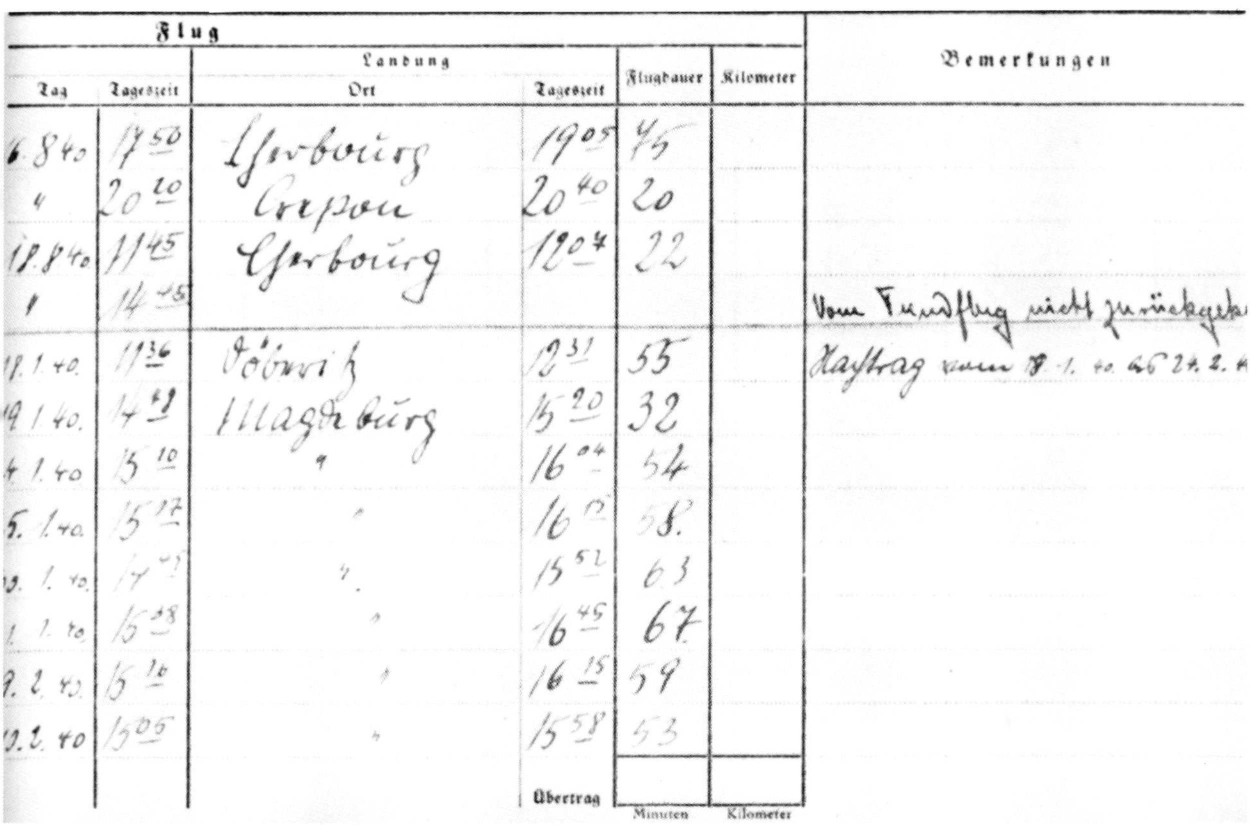

Flug						Bemerkungen
		Landung				
Tag	Tageszeit	Ort	Tageszeit	Flugdauer	Kilometer	
6.8.40	17 50	Cherbourg	19 05	75		
"	20 20	Crepon	20 40	20		
18.8.40	11 45	Cherbourg	12 07	22		
"	14 45					Vom Feindflug nicht zurückge[illegible]
18.1.40	11 36	Döberitz	12 31	55		Haftrag vom 8.1.40 bis 24.2.[illegible]
19.1.40	14 48	Magdeburg	15 20	32		
[illegible]4.1.40	15 10	"	16 04	54		
[illegible]5.1.40	15 17	"	16 15	58		
[illegible].1.40	14 49	"	15 52	63		
[illegible]1.1.40	15 38	"	16 45	67		
[illegible]9.2.40	15 16	"	16 15	59		
[illegible]9.2.40	15 05	"	15 58	53		
			Übertrag	Minuten	Kilometer	

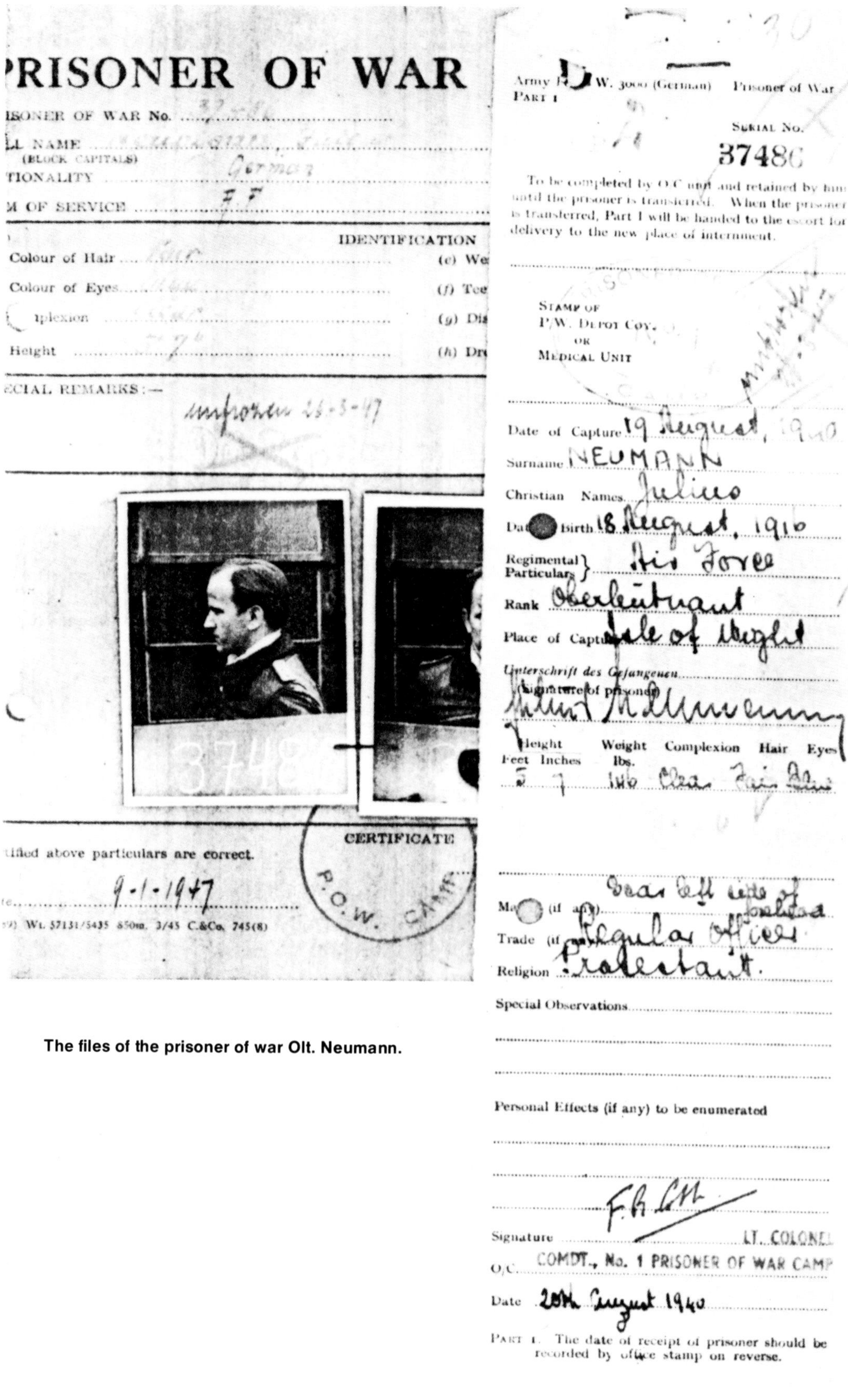

PRISONER OF WAR

PRISONER OF WAR No. 37486

FULL NAME [illegible]
(BLOCK CAPITALS)

NATIONALITY German

ARM OF SERVICE [illegible]

IDENTIFICATION

Colour of Hair Fair

Colour of Eyes Blue

Complexion [illegible]

Height 5' 7"

(e) We[illegible]

(f) Tee[illegible]

(g) Dis[illegible]

(h) Dr[illegible]

SPECIAL REMARKS:— [illegible] 26-3-47

3748

CERTIFICATE

Certified above particulars are correct.

Date 9-1-1947

P.O.W. CAMP

(39) Wt. 57131/5435 850m. 3/45 C.&Co. 745(8)

Army Form W. 3000 (German) Prisoner of War
Part I

Serial No.
3748C

To be completed by O.C unit and retained by him until the prisoner is transferred. When the prisoner is transferred, Part I will be handed to the escort for delivery to the new place of internment.

Stamp of P/W. Depot Coy. or Medical Unit

Date of Capture 19 August, 1940

Surname NEUMANN

Christian Names Julius

Date of Birth 18 August, 1916

Regimental Particulars } Air Force

Rank Oberleutnant

Place of Capture Isle of Wight

Unterschrift des Gefangenen
(Signature of prisoner)

Height Feet	Height Inches	Weight lbs.	Complexion	Hair	Eyes
5	7	146	Clear	Fair	Blue

Marks (if any) Scar left side of [illegible]

Trade (if any) Regular Officer

Religion Protestant.

Special Observations

Personal Effects (if any) to be enumerated

Signature LT. COLONEL

O/C. COMDT., No. 1 PRISONER OF WAR CAMP

Date 20th August 1940

Part I. The date of receipt of prisoner should be recorded by office stamp on reverse.

The files of the prisoner of war Olt. Neumann.

This trio of photos shows a German fighter making an emergency landing in Kent in August 1940. The landing was filmed by an English private citizen.

The Bf 109 comes in with its landing gear retracted

. . . touches down and continues sliding with its tail raised.

. . . and finally, after pivoting halfway around, comes to rest in a cloud of dust!

Fighters on patrol above the Channel.

Five kill markings decorate the rudder of Lt. Krug's aircraft from JG 26. Three French and two British aircraft fell victim to him.

The two strongest opponents of the Battle of Britain.

Genlt. a.D. Galland recently compared the two in this manner: "The modern Vickers-Supermarine Spitfire was 20-30km slower than the Bf 109, but definitely had an advantage in its turning ability. German guns and ammunition were markedly superior to their British counterparts. Another advantage was that the DB engines were fuel injected instead of having carburetors, which means they didn't quit while pulling negative g's at the critical moment in a dogfight. When being pursued, the English fighters would normally attempt to get away by performing a split S, a half roll, and then a half loop, whereas we would simply give it full throttle and press straight on with our eyes bulging out of their sockets."

During the last third of the Battle most of the raids were flown at night. All aircraft, even the He 111 of Fw. Boos, were painted in a night camouflage.

This aircraft from KG 26 carries a "fat loaf" over the Channel.

A dramatic moment for the crew of a bomber. This He 111 was forced to ditch after being shot down by an "Anson." Leaving a long trail of oil and fuel behind it, the aircraft comes to rest. Now it's a matter of getting the liferaft into the water as quick as possible and getting out of the sinking airplane.

After daytime losses became unbearable for the German bombers, most of the attacks occurred under the cover of darkness. A Ju 88 crew on a nighttime raid against England.

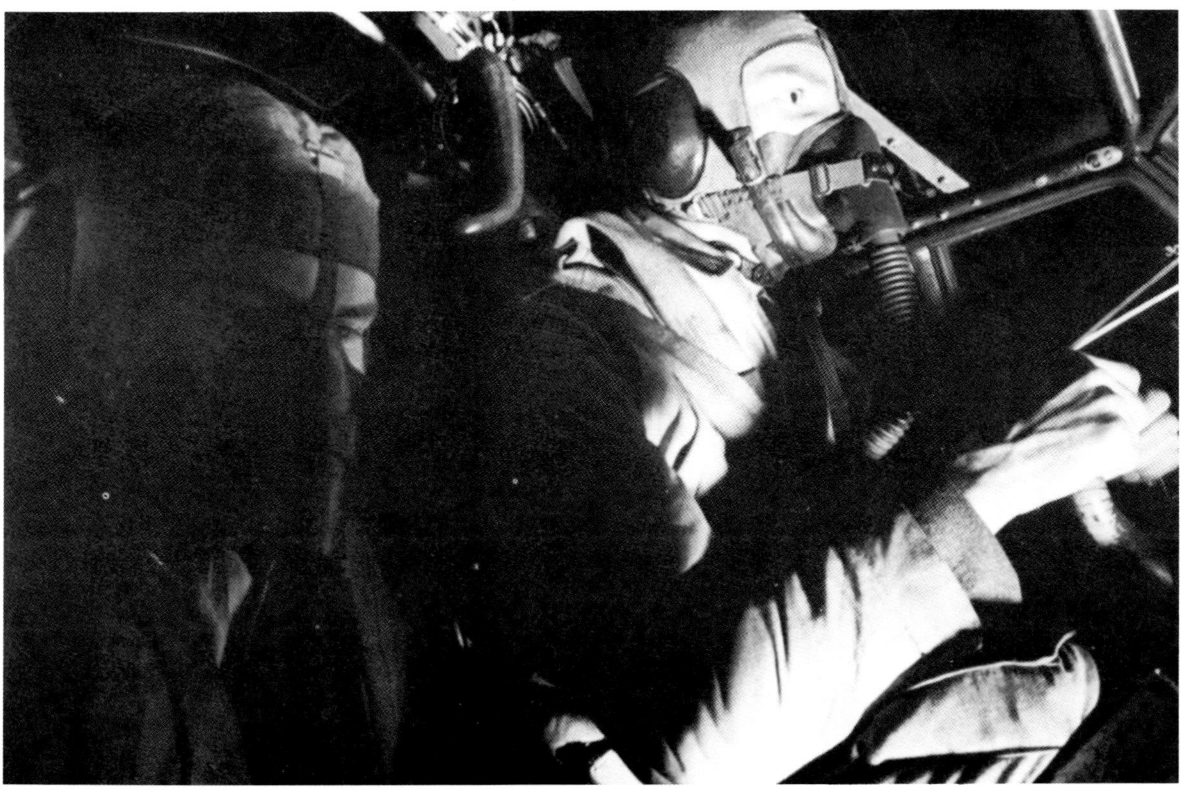

Propaganda was in full swing. Cameramen from a Luftwaffe propaganda company film a scramble at JG 26. In the weekly film broadcast only the cockpit and the boarding pilot can be seen. In actuality, the "pilot" is a mechanic.

The death of German pilots continues. Even Peter Göring, a nephew of the Reichsmarschall, and Paul Galland, Adolf Galland's youngest brother, join the ranks of fallen pilots; left to right: Lt. Paul Galland, Hptm. Clausen, and Hptm. Borris, who died during the defense of the Reich.

JG 2, which with JG 26 had to bear the brunt of air defense in the West after the Russian campaign began and units were withdrawn to the East, receives the new Fw 190A fighters.

Hptm. Hans "Assi" Hahn, commander of III/JG 2 "Richthofen", is greeted by his dog following a mission.

Major Walter Oesau, Wearer of the Swords to the Knight's Cross, takes some time to work in his garden, a rare picture of tranquility during these times. The Battle of Britain is over, but the air war in the West continues.

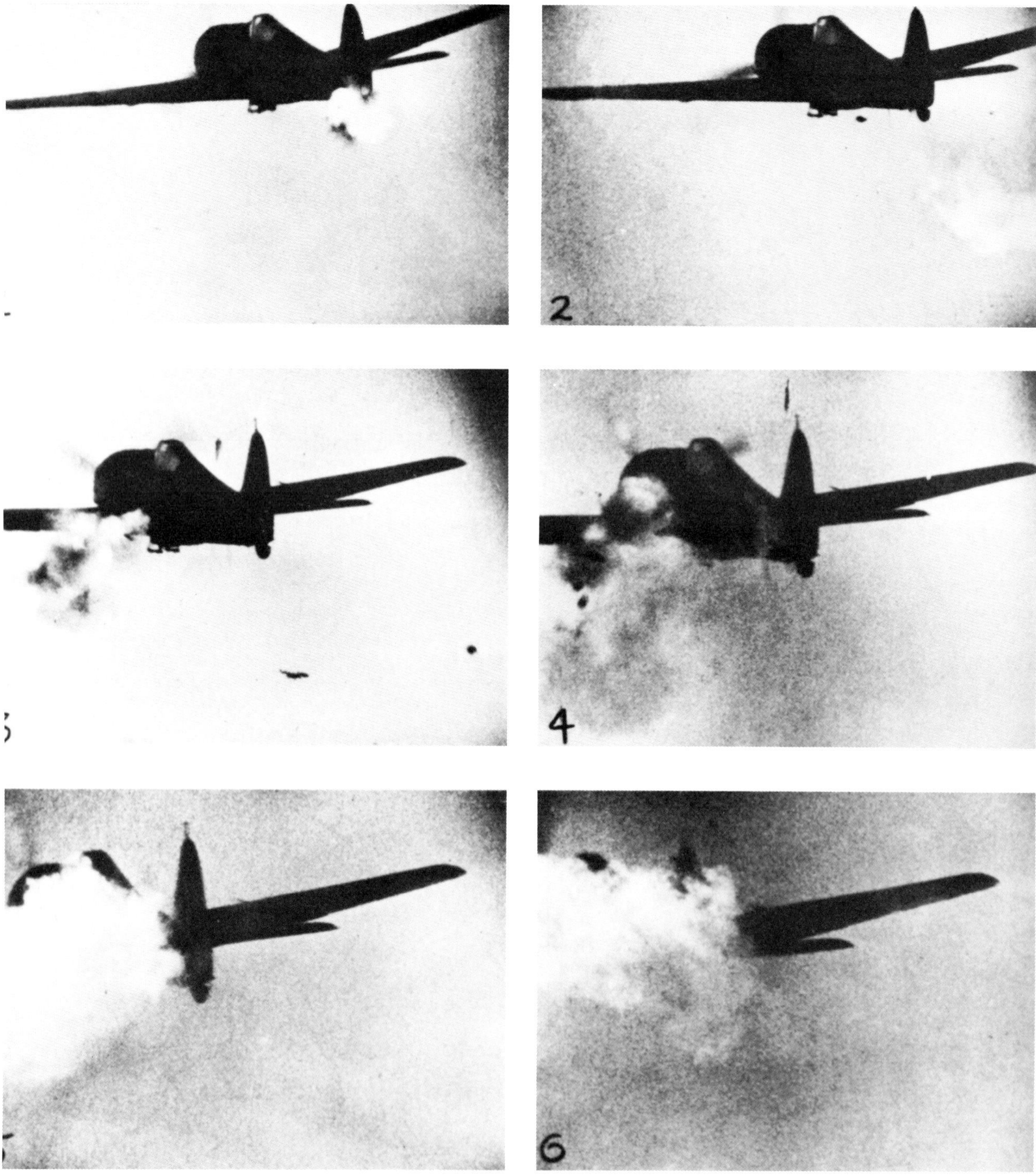

Since the increasing losses being suffered by the bombers on daylight missions could not be curtailed, fighters were equipped with bomb racks and assumed the role of daylight bombing. These tactics, however, were unsuccessful, primarily because not enough fighters were employed. These photos, taken from the gun camera of a British fighter, show the final moments of an Fw 190 fighter-bomber.

Ofw. Roth from 4/JG 26 sits on alert. Taking off from Brest-Morley, the fighters provide protection for the group of German warships.

The Luftwaffe enjoyed considerable success when it provided fighters, Zerstörer, and night fighters as air support for Operation "Donnerkeil und Cerberus." This operation involved the German battleships "Scharnhorst" and "Gneisenau", together with the heavy cruiser "Prinz Eugen", passing through the Channel under the very noses of the British.

A Bf 110 of II/ZG 76 is refuelled from a tanker so that it can quickly return to its duty of protecting the group of ships in the Channel.

A Bf 110 overflies the "Gneisenau", which is steaming at top speed towards the east.

In spite of all the successes and sacrifices of the German troops, the Battle of Britain was a futile one, since Hitler had no serious intentions of carrying out Operation "Seelöwe" - the invasion of England. The many thousands of dead, wounded, and captured were the victims of an attempt, doomed from the beginning, to single-handedly drive England from the skies.

THE BATTLE FOR THE MEDITERRANEAN

After the war spilled over into the Balkans in April of 1941, the Luftwaffe used the airfields of friendly Bulgaria as its jumping-off point. The target was Yugoslavia and Greece, which had been occupied by the British in the interim. From this limited theater of the war developed the expansive North African campaign. A bitter tragedy lay in the fact that the German High Command viewed the Mediterranean and North African theaters as having little importance, even though victories in these areas could have made a decisive change in the war's outcome.

What would have happened had Rommel taken Egypt with his Afrika Korps and continued on into Persia? By doing so he would have blocked a supply route used by the Allies later in the war; for it was through the Suez Canal that Great Britain brought much of the raw materials from her colonies. The Soviet Union, facing a serious threat in 1941/1942, depended on American supplies crossing Persia from the Gulf. These supply lines, operated by such a large power so far from its own land, could have been placed in great jeopardy had German troops been effectively utilized.

Of course, this is all very hypothetical and there are already too many 'ifs' and 'buts' concerning the whole affair. We will therefore concentrate on the actual sequence of events. After the successful conclusion of the Balkan campaign with the capture of Greece, the island of Crete was invaded. The invasion of this island was the largest single airborne operation undertaken up to that time. This victory, however, was bought at the price of a high amount of casualties suffered by the airborne troops and transport pilots. Aside from Crete there was the possibility of taking Malta. But Mussolini held back and didn't permit his troops to invade Malta. This was another example of how the fascist leader underestimated his own possibilities, for there was never even any attempt by the Italians to attack the important island fortress of Malta during the entire war. It should be added that Rommel, too, underestimated the danger Malta posed for his operations.

German troops landed in the North African theater on the 12th of February, 1941, in Tripoli. With this was born the Afrika Korps, which very soon developed into a tough opponent for the British troops. The Luftwaffe played an important role in the victories of these outstanding forces. Men such as Helbig and Marseille had a reputation which went beyond their own troops and those of the Axis.

In Africa the 88mm flak gun was finally able to demonstrate its abilities as an anti-tank weapon. Halder, and others like him, must answer for the victory that was denied to the soldiers of the Heer and their fellow combatants in the Luftwaffe. As the responsible commanding officer for the North African area, he declared it to be a secondary theater of operations - and by doing so effectively cut off the necessary support. Hitler's twisted idea that Russia could be conquered in a few short months must have certainly influenced this decision.

A Bf 109 of II/JG 27 with the Berlin Bear as its coat of arms, at the Belica airfield in Bulgaria - summer 1941.

A colorful collection of German Luftwaffe aircraft: Bf 109s, Ju 87s, and Do 17s.

Even Zerstörer from II/ZG 26 "Horst Wessel", the "Holzschuhgruppe" (wooden shoe Gruppe), are involved. The coat of arms, a wooden shoe, is prominent on the yellow painted nose; nearby are Messerschmitt fighters from II/JG 27.

Also a participant in the Balkan campaign is StG 2 "Immelmann", which I Gruppe can be seen here. A Scottish terrier in a white circle, seen on the side of this Ju 87 B-2, was the unit's coat of arms.

The commander of StG 2, Otl. Dr. Kupfer, Wearer of the Oak Leaves to the Knight's Cross, sits in his aircraft; below right is the upper part of the wing's coat of arms, the Shield of the Teutonic Order.

The Balkan campaign is over. Gfm. von Brauchitsch, the commanding officer of the Heer, has arrived in Athens via Ju 52 to accept the capitulation of Greece. During a short discussion under open skies at the airfield, his commanders brief him on the situation; left to right: Gen. Greifenberg, Gen. Stumme, Oberst Hesse, Gfm. von Brauchitsch.

The Reich war flag waves in the breeze next to the Greek national flag on the Acropolis in Athens.

7/JG 26 arrived in Sicily with their Bf 109 E-7s in the spring of 1941 - their target is North Africa.

Final briefing before takeoff. From the Athens airfield these Ju 88s of KG 76 will be taking off for operations in the Aegean.

A British frigate has been sighted and is under attack. It's part of a group of escorts bound for Crete.

In these days there were two critical targets for the combat pilots operating in the Mediterranean: Crete and Malta. The island of Malta was by far the more important. Its strategic value, however, was grossly underestimated by the General Staff of both the Luftwaffe and the Heer, an oversight that would soon have serious consequences.

So the war engulfed the island of Crete. Preparations involved heavy bombardment by the Luftwaffe. After a massive dogfight, a fighter aircraft of JG 77 was forced to land on the beach of Malemes on Crete.

A scant 100m further on lies the British opponent, a Hawker Hurricane.

On the morning of May 20th, 1941, paratroopers prepare to board their Ju 52 transports which will take them to Crete.

An anti-tank position somewhere in Crete's interior. For a long time the 37mm anti-tank gun was the heaviest caliber weapon that the paratroopers had available to them.

Losses suffered by the German paratroopers were enormously high in Crete. Many found their last resting place on Cretan soil, as did this paratrooper. This was also a reason why Hitler rejected the planned airborne operation against Malta.

The radioman on board a Bf 110 has just received an important radio message and passes it, along with the coordinates for the target area, to the pilot.

After receiving the message, the Schwarm leader's aircraft peels off onto a new course. Drop tanks under the wings provide increased range.

Cleared for takeoff! 3/JG 27 has received new mission orders and readies for takeoff.

This time it's fighter escort for the Ju 87s of StG 1. Their mission is already over;the 250kg bomb under the fuselage and the four 50kg bombs under the wings have been dropped.

The Fi 156 "Stork", used by the Wüstennotstaffel (Desert Rescue Squadrons), was often the last chance for many German and Allied fliers forced to land or parachute in the desert. Many owed their lives to the men of Hptm. Kroseberg, the commander of this particular squadron.

This photo demonstrates how well the camouflage paint blends into the natural surroundings.

The morale of the maintenance crews was constantly being put to the most severe test due to the working conditions and extreme temperatures. Without fail, however, they fulfilled all expectations and made possible the shining successes enjoyed by the fighter pilots in Africa.

Two Ju 87 R-2 of I/StG 1 overfly the Sicilian harbor at Trapani, in which a large number of German and Italian ships are docked. With drop tanks the Stukas could even reach the English convoys bound for Malta - May 1941.

A Ju 87 has crashed directly next to the Via Balbia, the main supply road for the Afrika Korps. Soldiers from a truck convoy rush to help.

Benghazi - a tiny barren settlement situated on the Mediterranean. During the campaign, Wehrmacht reports often contained references to this town.

The mosque of Martuba, a tiny desert haven. But in 1941 this name was on everyone's lips.

Drinking water! Whoever occupied an oasis with drinking water had a very important strategic advantage. In North Africa, both weapons and nature played a role in determining victory or defeat.

During the ground war in Africa, the 88mm flak gun played a major and often decisive role in battle. Sollum and Halfaya Pass are just two of the places successfully defended by the flak crewmen manning these massive guns.

Destroyed English tanks can be seen as specks in front of this flak emplacement; in the background is a dust devil.

One of the demolished British tanks, which didn't stand a chance against the high velocity, accuracy, and penetrating power of the 88mm flak gun.

A Ju 87 D-1 is loaded with bombs. Instead of the two ETCs under each wing carrying 50kg bombs, the pylons on these wings could carry a heavier load. This boosted the total bomb capacity on this Stuka version to 1800kg.

After takeoff from a nearby airfield a Bf 110 turns onto its course. Heer soldiers act as interested observers.

The airfield at Benina is littered with the remains of destroyed German aircraft; in the foreground is a Ju 88, and in the background to the right can be seen a Bf 110. Luftwaffe losses grew and grew, while the superiority of the English steadily increased.

Taking off on an escort mission over the Med. 2/JG 27 flies out to join up with a Ju 52 formation and provide fighter protection against enemy aircraft.

Leaving long trails of dust behind them, the rest of the Staffel takes off. Notice the distance between the aircraft, which keeps the blowing sand from obscuring the pilots' visibility.

The Ju 52/3m on its dangerous journey across the Mediterranean Sea. The fact that Malta was not prevented from being a base for the British fighters and bombers is now being felt. Because of this, 60% and more of the German supplies for the Afrika Korps were lost.

Happily, this formation of good old "Tante Ju's" makes it to the airport at Derna.

Having landed doesn't mean being out of danger. This Ju 52 burst into flames while being refuelled.

Often there's only scrap metal left over!

This Ju 52/3m brings wounded soldiers back from Africa to their native soil.

A confusing array of signs outside of the ruins of Bardia points the way for the soldiers of the Afrika Korps. Scenes like this could be found on every front.

The last single seat biplane used by one of the warring nations was the Italian Fiat CR 42 "Falco" fighter, used in Africa by the Regia Aeronautica (Italian Air Force).

NJG 2 operated from Sicily with its Ju 88 C-4 night fighters.

Olt. Hissbach's Ju 88 approaching the airfield. The antennae of the "Lichtenstein" radar system are easily recognized in front of the nose.

Bullet damage forced this Ju 88 of NJG 2 to make an emergency landing near the airbase of Cania. The nose armament can be made out quite clearly.

"Yellow 14", an aircraft recognized by friend and foe alike. It was flown by Olt. Hans Joachim Marseille.

Olt. Marseille discusses his latest dogfight with some of his comrades.

Recreation area of 3/JG 27, whose Staffelkapitän was Joachim Marseille.

Ordered to Africa as an Oberfähnrich in April 1941, Marseille enjoyed an unprecedented series of successes. Not without reason did Galland call him the virtuoso among fighter pilots.

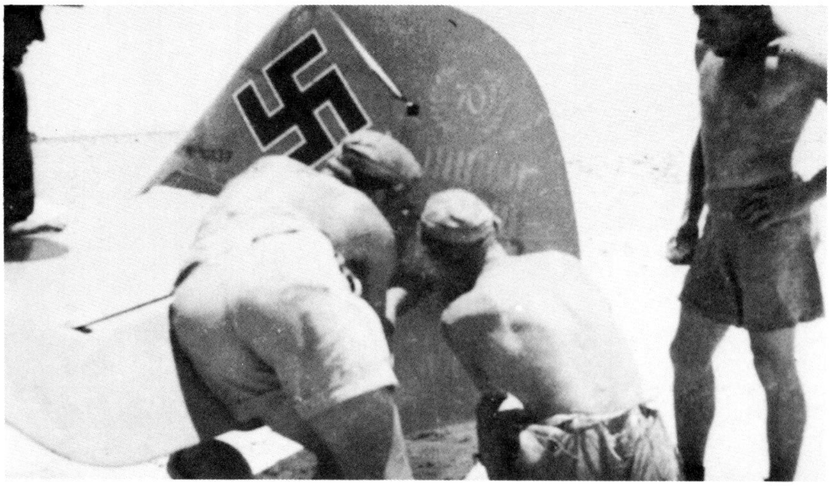

A new kill marking is painted on the rudder of Marseille's Bf 109. In spite of orders to the contrary, the pilots maintained this custom.

His youthful carefree attitude often caused headaches for his superiors, but his youthful charm remained forever in the memories of those who knew him.

Still victorious over his enemies, Hptm. Hans-Joachim Marseille died on October 30th, 1942. Even though his victories were exclusively limited to English, Australian, and New Zealander pilots, he quickly became the most successful pilot operating in the African theater. In February of 1942 he was awarded the Knight's Cross after his 50th victory. In September of the same year he received the Diamonds to the Knight's Cross award. 28 days later the engine on his new Bf 109 G-2 gave out without suffering any damage from enemy action. While bailing out, he struck the rudder of the aircraft and fell unconscious to his death without being able to open his parachute. The picture shows Major Eduard Neumann, the commander of JG 27 (Joachim Marseille's unit), paying his final respects to the youngest Hauptmann of the German Wehrmacht.

A weapons crewman has removed the MG 151/20, designed to fire through the propeller hub, from its Bf 109 F-2 and has disassembled it in preparation for cleaning. Not an easy task given the sandy surroundings.

The last rays of the rapidly sinking sun cast a peaceful glow upon this Bf 109 G-2, which serves such a sinister purpose.

The Battle of North Africa is almost lost. Me 323 "Gigant" (Giant) aircraft carry desperately needed supplies in their huge bellies, but their efforts are only a drop in a bucket. Too much is lost to the Malta-based British fighters on the route from Sicily to Tunisia.

A Spitfire, shot down on a North African beach. In spite of the pressing superiority of the Allied forces, German fighters are still able to rack up victories.

The Hs 129, called mockingly "The Can Opener" by landlubbers, was expected to support the hard-pressed ground troops in their fight against the superior numbers of English and American tanks. The situation becomes more and more critical.

Somewhere above the Mediterranean Sea a Ju 52/3 MS comes under attack from a British Beaufighter. To locate mines, the aircraft is equipped with a search ring mounted under the fuselage. This aircraft was used to locate and destroy mines.

The transport crews suffered considerably. More and more it became an accomplishment just to reach their destination, as this Ju 52 of KG zbV 1 managed to do. It is seen here together with Italian transports at the Derna airfield.

An aircraft was caught while making its way across the Med and had to ditch. While the pilot of the rescue plane eases up on the throttle, a medic prepares to drop a life raft out the floor hatch.

A Macchi C202 "Folgore" Italian fighter sits on an airfield in Sicily. When flown by experienced pilots, this aircraft was a worthy opponent. However, it arrived at the front units too late.

The end of the Afrika Korps. What can somehow be salvaged is flown out. Many destroyed aircraft are left behind. Of the soldiers, only the Spezialisten (specialists) can be evacuated, since there is very little transport room available and the enemy is rapidly approaching the last remaining intact airfields.

Germany has lost the war in North Africa. III/JG 27 makes a turbulent retreat back to Sicily.

It was all for nothing. Even the use of the large Ju 290 transport, which destroyed fuselage provides a seat for these American GIs in Bizerte, couldn't provide the necessary supplies.

In a well-deserved break the "black men" of 3/JG 27 relax in the midday sun - Evreux 1943.

In the meantime, the pilots of JG 27 have arrived in Evreux, France, and make preparation for the difficult task that lies ahead - the defense of the Reich; right to left: Ofw. Reiner Pöttgen, who flew as Joachim Marseille's wingman, Fw. Geisinger, unknown, Matthias, the black servant of Marseille who voluntarily remained with the Geschwader, and Ofw. Krämer, who, like all the rest, belonged to 3/JG 27.

Scramble! American aircraft are reported outbound from Africa. This means that German fighters stationed in Sicily are needed.

Together as a Schwarm the Bf 109 G-6s lift off the runway.

But the German defensive might has already been weakened by the huge expansion of the European theater of operations. A Bf 110 of ZG 76 lies in ruins on the airfield of Monteco-ruino in Sicily.

During a scramble this pilot of 1/JG 27 had difficulties with his engine and couldn't get enough altitude to avoid ramming into a hangar.

JG 53 also operated out of Sicily and, along with other units, attempted to stop the influx of American bombers.

THE LUFTWAFFE'S VERDUN - THE RUSSIAN CAMPAIGN

Due to the ever expanding fronts the Geschwader found themselves being broken up. The area covered by a single Staffel took on enormous proportions. Geschwader of all types were removed from the Channel front and deployed on the Eastern Front as early as the beginning of Operation Barbarossa - the Russian campaign. This had the effect of permitting the RAF to recover and switch from defensive to offensive tactics, which cost the civilian population of Germany plenty of sleep in the truest sense of the word. For the air defense in the West was borne by only two units: JG 1 and JG 26. But the dismantling of the air front against England didn't fully meet the demand for men and material on the Eastern Front. There were simply not enough aircraft and crews available to fill the constantly expanding areas in the East. Soon the Luftwaffe, and here especially the bombers, were no longer in a position to follow any type of clear strategic concept. Russian tanks were chopped up piecemeal by bombers and Stukas, but the Russians cranked their replacements out by the dozens from hastily constructed factories a few hundred kilometers to the East. Now, more than ever, the absence of a four engine long range bomber was sorely felt by the Luftwaffe.

Beginning at the end of 1942, the units of the Luftwaffe increasingly became tasked with direct support of the Heer, whose initial elan began to take a beating from the vast distances of the Eastern Front and sharply rising resistance of the Soviet troops. The bombers and Stukas began to divide their power into individual, single sorties. German fighter pilots watched their victory tallies skyrocket; for every Russian plane that was shot down, three or four more sprang up far to the East, out of reach of the bombers - or were delivered from the USA and England via the port of Murmansk. The Luftwaffe, on the other hand, was hardly able to maintain the minimum strength of its Geschwader in the East; beginning in 1943 the air defense over the German homeland demanded more and more pilots. Both the personnel and technical aspects of the operation suffered from these shortages. Whereas the Luftwaffe had absolute air superiority over Russia in 1941 and the first half of 1942, the tables gradually began to turn - to the disadvantage of the Germans. On the one hand, it was due to the increase in supplies provided by the Allies; on the other hand, the Russians brought their homemade aircraft to the Front, which were increasingly able to hold their own against the Germans, especially their fighters.

Even if the Russian Air Force was never able to take matters into its own hands in the East, the Luftwaffe still found itself being pushed on the defensive more and more. The enormous successes achieved by Hartmann, Barkhorn, Rall and all the many others of JG 3, 51, 52, 53, or 54 were not enough to stem the flood of Russian airplanes. The technically antiquated, short range bomber Geschwader had just as little success in stopping the river of Soviet supply columns. And just as the German Heer bled itself dry at the gates of Verdun in 1916/1917, so was the case of the Luftwaffe in the vast expanse of Russia.

As the sun rose in the east on the morning of June 22, 1941, a massive armada of bombers, fighters, Stukas and Zerstörer flew toward her - the German Luftwaffe had opened the Russian Campaign. He 111 aircraft of KG 53 could be found in the first attack wave.

Neatly lined up in rows, the obsolete I-15 Soviet fighters were destroyed in great numbers at the beginning of the offensive.

After the first attack wave of German aircraft had disappeared from the skies above the Soviet airfields, the wrecks of airplanes lay strewn about under the morning sun.

Major Hannes Trautloft, commander of the famous JG 54, seen here in the best of spirits.

A view into the cockpit of a Bf 109 fighter.

The commander prepares to take off. Below the cockpit can be seen the insignia of JG 54 - a green heart. This symbol had its origins in Major Trautloft's homeland of Thuringia, which was called the green heart of Germany.

A Russian Ilyushin Il-2 combat aircraft. This type was heavily armored and was notorious for being able to take a considerable amount of punishment.

Russian I-16 "Rata" fighters on a Russian grass field in the central part of the Eastern Front.

JG 3, which received its nickname after the suicide of Generalluftzeugmeister Udet, also fought in the East. This is the aircraft of the technical officer of the third Gruppe.

Fighter pilots who became famous during the Russian campaign; left is Hptm. Günther Rall, to the right is Maj. Hans Philip.

An He 111 of KG 55 is loaded with an 1800kg bomb.

On November 17th, 1941, 9/KG 55 attacked the railyards of Valuyki, bombing from an altitude of 4300m. Large columns of smoke indicate the accuracy of the attack.

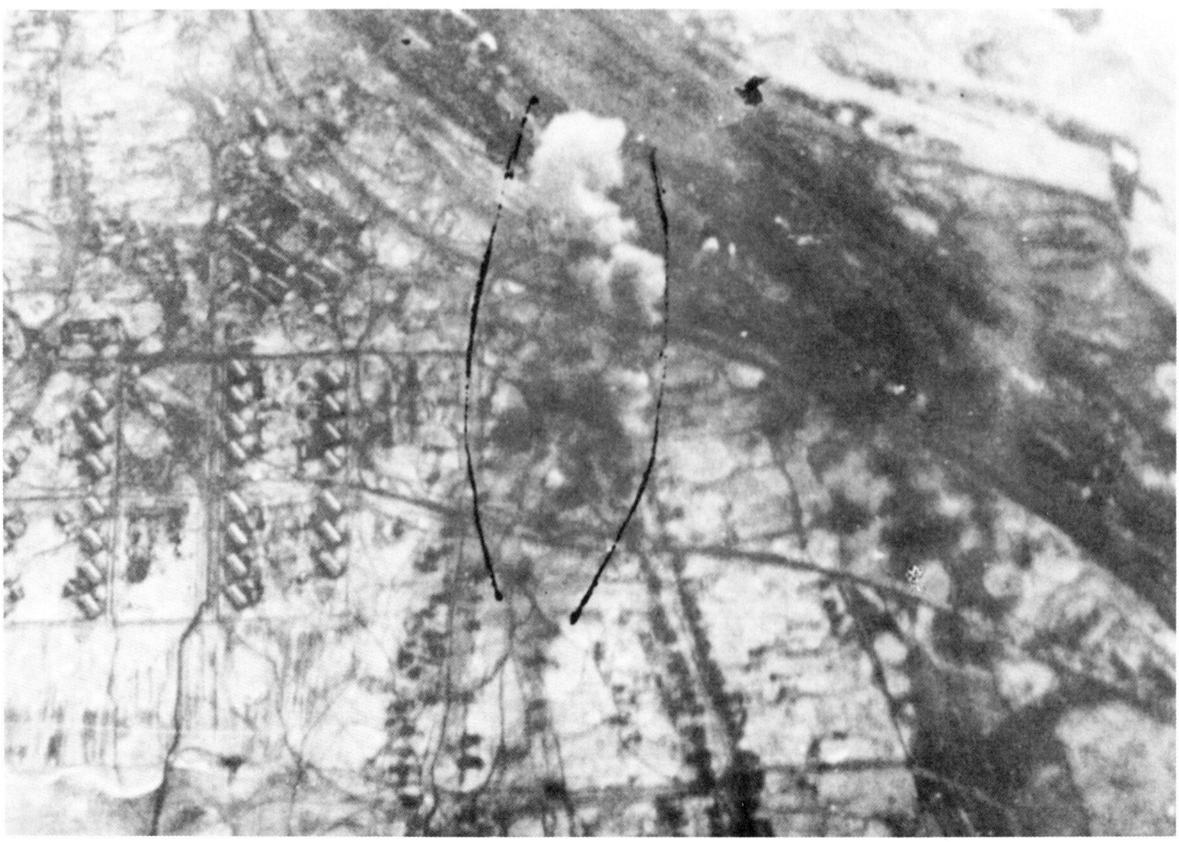

The He 111 flown by Fw. Johann Boos sustained flak damage, and due to the shot-out landing gear hydraulics, was forced to crash land.

Fw. Boos, who was awarded the Knight's Cross in 1943 while in a prisoner-of-war camp, brought back some "souvenirs" from this mission, too.

Relaxing moments such as this scene from JG 3 "Udet", with accordian and cheerful tunes, are seldom found.

The situation can change lightning fast. Russian combat aircraft have attacked the parking area of I/JG 51 and have destroyed several airplanes. A crewman, who had been working on the aircraft in the foreground, has been killed. His lifeless body still lies next to the fuselage.

The Luftwaffe began to employ new types of aircraft to counter the growing strength of the Russian tank force. These are Henschel ground attack aircraft. The airplane in the foreground is an Hs 129 A-0, still equipped with Argus engines, whereas the aircraft in the background is equipped with the production Gnome-Rhone engines. The Hs 129 was armed with four machine guns and from one to four bombs, depending on weight.

For a time Italian fighters, such as these Macchi C 200, were also deployed to Russia. These aircraft have just arrived in Kiev.

The MG 17 guns of a Bf 110 are being loaded. This was a procedure that required a great amount of care in order to prevent jamming.

While the batteries are being charged, last minute repairs are made to the radioman's equipment.

The Geschwader adjutant takes off on a test flight. In front of the Geschwader's coat of arms can be seen the insignia for the third Gruppe, the cross of Jesau.

"Yellow Two", of 6/JG 3 was forced to make a belly landing short of the airfield at Vaborovna. A cavalry battalion brought the pilot back to his unit.

He 111 H aircraft from KG 53, "Legion Condor", wearing white camouflage to disguise themselves from Russian fighters, approach a Russian troop concentration.

The commander of an attack Gruppe taxis for takeoff. Due to the snow the landing gear covers over the wheels have been removed. The camouflage pattern is a field-applied version.

Winter has arrived! Temperatures of 20, 30, or even 50 degrees celsius below zero, accompanied by snowstorms of up to 100 kilometers per hour, often brought flight operations to a standstill. This type of situation demanded everything of the flying and technical personnel.

More and more accidents during takeoff and landings were caused by iced-over tarmac. This time a Bf 110 of ZG 26 and a Bf 109 of JG 52 have crashed into each other.

A heating cart is used to warm up the engines. Otherwise a takeoff would be unthinkable.

Bombs of all sizes are loaded into an He 111 H of KG 53. Notice that the propellers are already turning over on A1+AH.

In the summer of 1943 Lt. Nowotny of 9/JG 54 had to make an emergency landing while returning from a mission. His aircraft suffered hits in the fuselage fuel tank and rear part of the cockpit. In making the emergency landing, he plowed into a flak emplacement and flipped his aircraft. Nowotny was awarded the Diamonds to the Knight's Cross in October of 1943.

Stukas of the "Immelmann" Geschwader could be found just about everywhere. They were quite often used as "firemen", pushing the enemy back wherever they had broken through.

The Ju 88, seen here from KG 76 based in Kursk, was probably the most versatile aircraft in the Luftwaffe. This aircraft demonstrated its worth in Russia and during the attacks on convoys in the Baltic and Mediterranean.

A successful Ju 88 pilot. Stabsfeldwebel Rudolf Nacke of III/KG 76 was personally awarded the Knight's Cross on July 23rd, 1941, by the commander-in-chief of the Luftwaffe, Hermann Göring.

Takeoff of II/ZG 26 in support of the hard-pressed ground forces. The Bf 110 in Russia had notable successes as a ground attack aircraft.

A busy day at this airfield as a formation of Hs 123s peels off for landing.

A successful pilot "beats up" the airfield, waggling the wings of his aircraft.

An Il-2 Russian combat aircraft, shot down by fighters of JG 52.

The remains of a Soviet Pe-2 light attack aircraft.

In the vastness of the Russian steppes all forward airfields looked the same. Improvisation was the order of the day; the airfield of JG 2 at Rogan near Charkov - 1943.

This collection of tents of KG 55 looks more like a medieval encampment than a forward airfield in the twentieth century. Among this cluster can be found the command post, the sleeping quarters, a field hospital, and repair facilities.

 As on all the other fronts, the Ju 52 bore the brunt of transport operations in Russia.

The losses suffered through enemy action and accidents caused a rapid decline in the capacities of the transport units.

A Ju 87 D of StG 2, "Immelmann" approaches a new target. The 50kg bombs underneath the wings and the 250kg bomb beneath the fuselage can be seen to good advantage.

A hit - as the Ju 87 (upper right) pulls up sharply following a successful strike, the pontoon bridge put up by the Russians during the night is blown up.

Major Brändle, Wearer of the Oak Leaves to the Knight's Cross and commander of III/JG 3, ponders the situation. The airspaces which the individual Gruppen and Geschwader now have to defend have become too large.

The Bf 109 G-2s of I/JG 3 stand ready for takeoff on the runway of Rogan.

A fighter Rotte taking off - the aircraft in the foreground clearly shows the unit markings: beneath the canopy is the green heart of JG 54 and next to that is the coat of arms with the cross of Jesau, the markings of III Gruppe. On the engine cover is the insignia of 7 Staffel, the flying wooden shoe.

The cannon of a Russian aircraft lying in a harvested sunflower field is evidence of a German fighter's latest aerial victory.

Waggling his wings, the pilot of this Bf 109 announces his latest victory to his comrades on the ground.

With the help of some companions, the crash site of the enemy is pinpointed; since the shootdown occurred without witnesses, the enemy aircraft's remains must be found in order to prove that it was actually a kill.

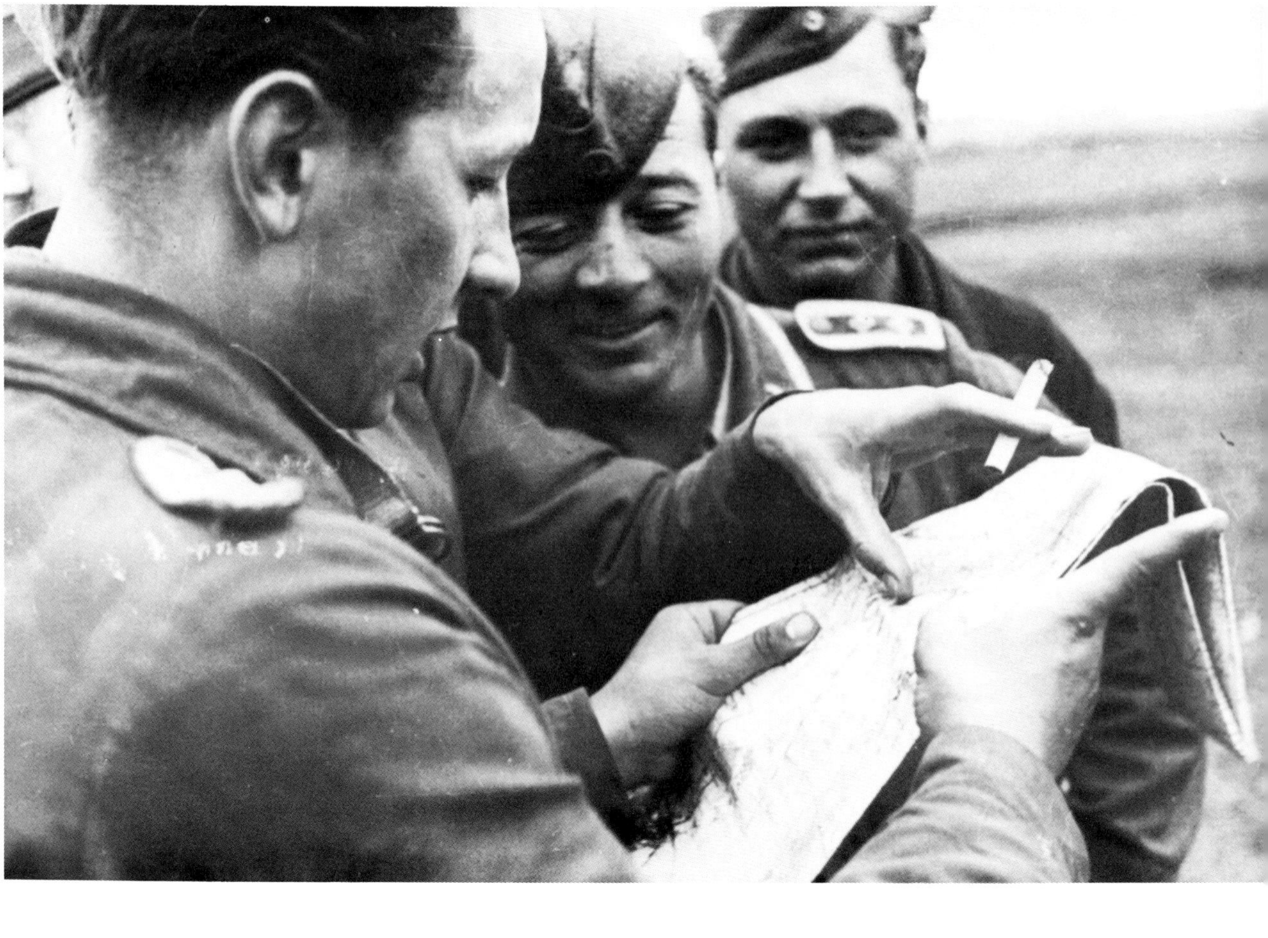

The strain of the recent dogfight still shows in the face of Lt. Ullmann, who is seen here reporting his kill.

Fighters and Stukas bore a heavy burden in fulfilling their ever-growing and increasingly difficult responsibilities in the vastness of Russia.

Maj. Hans-Ulrich Rudel, left, and Olt. Erich Hartmann, both Wearers of the Diamonds to the Knight's Cross of the Iron Cross, were the Eastern Front's most successful pilots in their respective branches - the Stukas and the fighters.

The Ju 88s of KG 76 approaching. The aircraft fly in Ketten (lit., links of a chain) comprised of three aircraft; these aircraft here are still forming up.

Shortly before peeling off to attack, the bombers assume this formation. Like its smaller sister the Ju 87, the Ju 88 was also capable of dive bombing.

Developed especially for ground attack, primarily against armor, the Hs 129 was often the last resort for stopping Russian tanks that had broken through the lines. Aside from the four machine guns, this type also carried a cannon mounted in a weapons tray underneath the fuselage.

Even the Fw 190, originally designed as a fighter, was successfully employed in ground attack operations. Four bombs could be mounted on this special fuselage ETC. The bomb in the left of the picture has the so called Jericho whistles fixed between its guidance fins. As the bomb fell, it made an infernal whistling noise which had a tremendous psychological effect.

Russian attack aircraft have appeared over an airfield once again and begin to riddle it with bombs and guns. This is a job for the 20mm flak guns.

One of the Il-2s has been hit. Its rudder has fallen to earth near the runway.

The Ju 88 in the foreground, piloted by Schwarm leader Lt. Ebersbach of KG 76, overflies the broad Volga riverbed south of Stalingrad.

Stalingrad is reached - the Ju 88 Gruppe flies away from one of the southern suburbs toward the heart of the city.

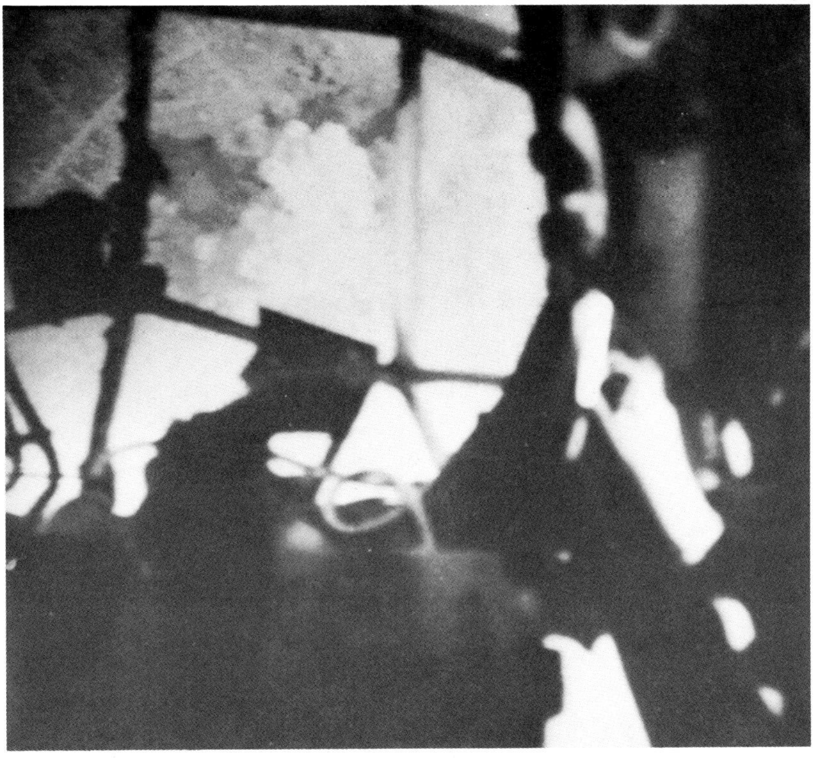

Diving steeply toward the hotly contested center of Stalingrad, the tank and tractor factory "Red October." During the attack dive the observer, Olt. Kempf, was able to take this extraordinary photo.

Happy to have avoided both flak and fighters, a course is set for the airbase. It will be reached in time to watch the setting sun.

146 Not everything goes as smoothly, such as this landing at KG 76's airfield of Pelykolodes. Crippled from shell damage in both engines as well as a defective landing gear, the aircraft crashlanded.

An imposing photograph of the Caucasus Mountains with the highest peak, the Elbrus, in the center.

An Fw 190 A-4 of I/JG 54 landing at a snowy airfield in Russia.

Flight operations on the water! I/JG 54 turned the Ivan Lake near Velikiye-Luki into a runway during the January days of 1942.

An unknown dead pilot. It was often only a matter of minutes from the indescribably wonderful feeling of free flight above the clouds to a horrible death in a plummeting, uncontrollable aircraft.

In the first Kesselschlachten (lit. "pocket battles"), where German troops found themselves encircled, the Luftwaffe's transport units played an important role. Like these Ju 52s above Demyansk, they supplied the trapped soldiers from the air.

Transport gliders, such as these Go 242s, were able to carry large amounts of goods to the troops without risking the loss of valuable transport aircraft.

The Me 321 could carry the heaviest of loads, even armored vehicles. Several aircraft were needed in order to get such a large and heavy bird into the air. The He 111 Z was built expressly for this purpose by joining two aircraft together at the wings and creating a five-engine "twin airplane." One is seen here taking off with an Me 321.

Some really big loaves! 1800kg bombs waiting to be loaded into two Ju 88 A-4s, headquarters aircraft of II/KG 54.

A Russian tank battalion has broken through the German lines and is threatening the supply columns. A task for the Ju 88s of KG 54 is to stop the Russian tanks with a direct attack.

Low-level attack of a Russian railyard, through which must pass the enemy's supplies. Although the branch line on the left has been completely destroyed by direct hits, the switching yard with its tanker cars on the right is left unscathed - a sure prize for the advancing German forces.

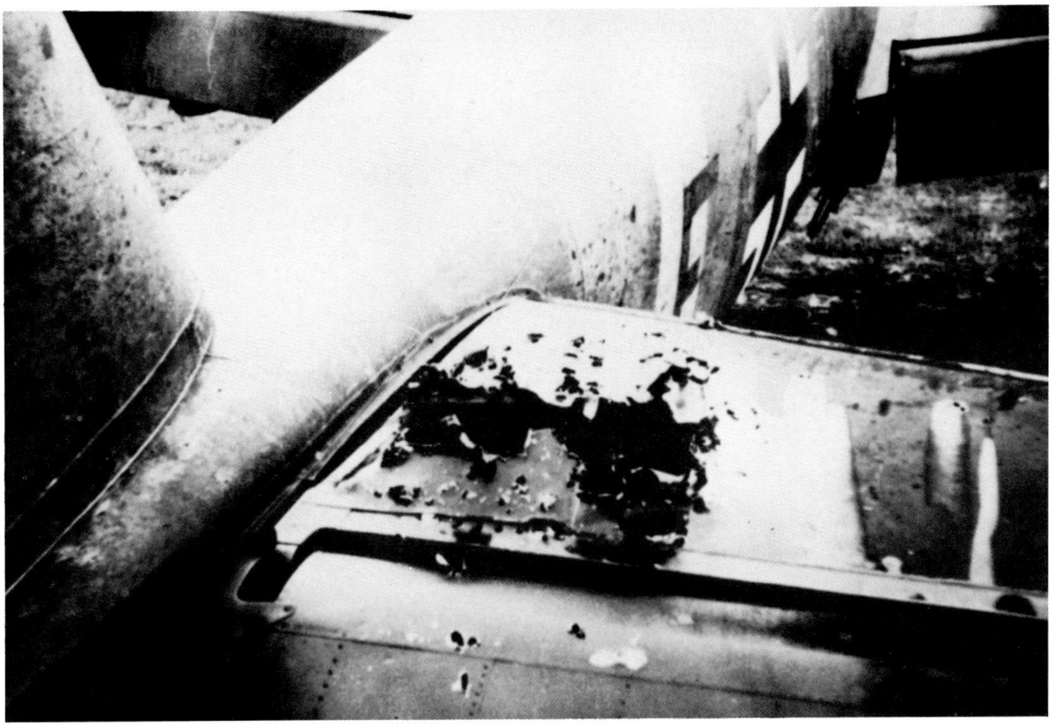

The crew of this aircraft was fortunate. Had the flak hit been a bit larger it would have knocked out the right horizontal stabilizer, which could lead to rather serious consequences.

The crew station of the radio operator on a Ju 88 A-4; to the left can be seen one of the two MG 81 machine guns, beneath the gun is the FuG 16 radio.

Hptm. Gerhard Barkhorn, commander of II/JG 52, is cleared for takeoff in his Bf 109 G-6. After Hartmann, he is the most successful fighter pilot in the world with 301 kills.

Another successful pilot of JG 52, of which Hartmann was also a member, is Hptm. Günther Rall with 250 aerial victories. He led III/JG 52. In this photo his ground crew is congratulating him on his 200th victory.

Maj. Brändle monitors the removal of his aircraft's DB 605 engine. He is visibly pleased.

When one has the misfortune of having to sit on alert when the noontime temperature reaches 30 degrees Celsius in the shade, one improvises - as this pilot of JG 3 apparently has done in Russia during the summer of 1943.

The Fw 190F proved to be a true workhorse, being used by the pilots of attack units.

Takeoff of an Fw 190F with a 250kg bomb hung beneath its fuselage. After dropping its bomb, the airplanes would then fly fighter protection for the Stukas.

In the far North - from Norway and Finland on down -there took place a bitter air war against the Allied supply routes in the North Sea. These routes were used by British and American ship convoys to bring necessary supplies to the Russians via the only ice-free Russian port in the North, Murmansk.

Bombers of KG 26, "Löwengeschwader" (Lion Geschwader) fly over the Finnish coastal areas on their way to Murmansk. These attacks were feared by the bomber crews because of the heavy concentrations of flak batteries in and around the harbor city.

The fighters of JG 5, "Eismeer" (Arctic Sea), provide the attackers with the necessary protection during the dangerous journey above the tundra of Finland and Russia. Even an emergency landing or a bailout could spell death in this wilderness.

The long-range reconnaissance and combat aircraft known as the Fw 200 "Condor" operated from their airbases in Norway. These dramatic photos were made during an attack on an Allied convoy in the North Sea. An Fw 200 has been severely damaged by ship anti-aircraft fire and is forced to ditch. As the convoy makes its way along in the background, the crew climbs out of the slowly sinking aircraft. In the lower picture, crew members can be seen inflating a life raft to pick up those comrades still in the water.

Maj. Werner Baumbach, Wearer of the Swords to the Knight's Cross, was, together with his KG 30 very successful in attacking the convoys.

A Ju 88 from KG 30 returns to its airfield after a successful mission. A special camouflage pattern was used for those aircraft operating over water.

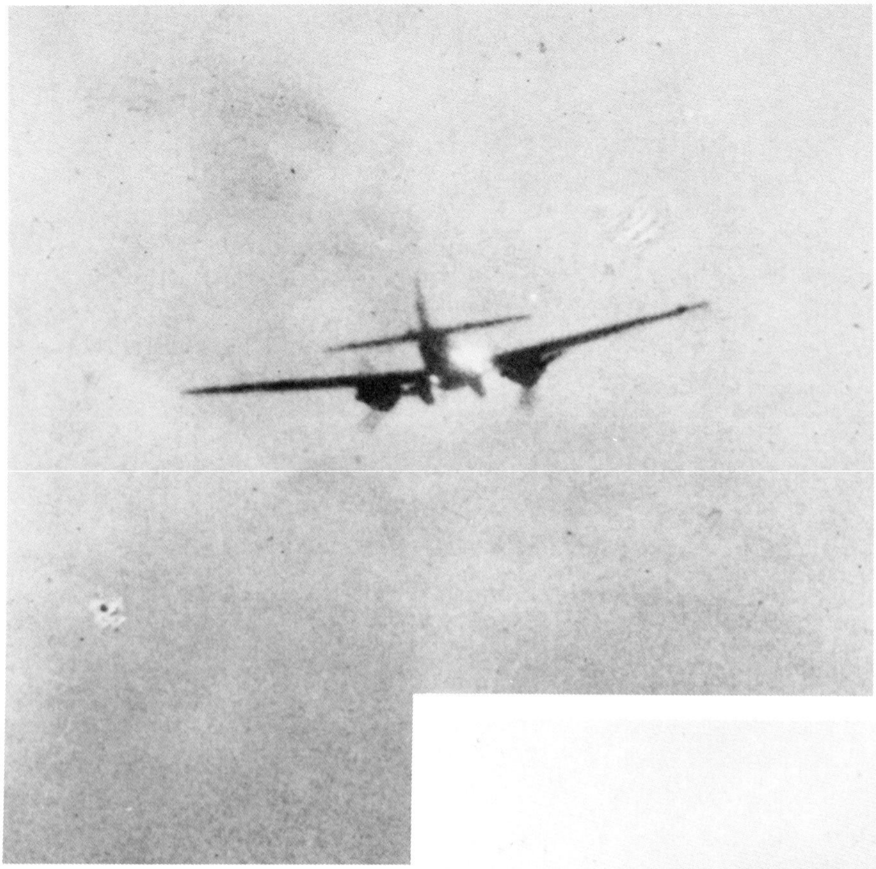

Many never returned from their missions over the ocean. This photo is taken from a Beaufighter, a British torpedo bomber and long-range fighter. As it attacks this Ju 88, hits can be seen striking in the wing root.

The end of a German aircraft crew. As a mushroom cloud of smoke rises from the burning oil slick on the water, the British fighter circles above the crash site. The aircraft can be seen to the right of the smoke column, about halfway up.

THE DEFENSE OF THE REICH - AIR WAR OVER GERMAN SOIL

Prior to the begin of the Russian Campaign in the summer of 1941, Geschwader after Geschwader was deployed from the Channel front to the East in the approach areas to the Soviet Union. This led to a total change in the air war in the West. The German Luftwaffe was forced to switch from an offensive to a defensive posture. In a reversal of roles, the British bomber operations intensified greatly -initially against targets in the occupied territories and shortly followed by attacks on the Reich. These attacks from the British Isles only really became a serious threat once the 8th USAAF arrived in England and began to carry out daylight bombing, while the RAF switched to night attacks. From this time on the severity and number of bomber raids grew consistently. The Luftwaffe was too preoccupied with the East and reacted too late and with too little intensity.

At this time the weaknesses in the top leadership of the Luftwaffe became readily apparent. Men such as Göring or Milch proved themselves to be incapable of providing the Luftwaffe with the support it so urgently required. They remained silent when it became apparent that changes were necessary in Hitler's prosecution of the air war. Göring, who once boasted proudly that he could be called Meier if an enemy plane ever crossed the borders of the Reich, did nothing to accept responsibility for the drastically changing conditions; in deference to Hitler's thinking, he did nothing to make the desperately needed improvements in the Jagdwaffe. And his deputy, Milch, was no different. In mid-1941, for example, he restricted the development of new engines with the ignorant comment: ". . . we don't need any new engines. The Führer has assured me that the war will be over with by autumn!" Even such a man with integrity as Ernst Udet was not in a position to meet the challenges of his position as Generalluftzeugmeister of Development and Procurement. Thus he sacrificed the concept of a four-engine strategic bomber (proposed by General Wever, first Generalstabschef of the Luftwaffe) in favor of the temporarily successful idea of the Stuka.

Particularly shocking was the fact that the wildly extravagant military and ministerial bureaucracy - either through shortsightedness or through incompetence - ignored the requests from the front lines for new developments. The Reichsluftministerium (Reich Air Ministry), or RLM for short, played an especially infamous role in this context. For example, as late as 1944 the RLM continued to allow the private and state-owned aircraft manufacturers to feud over new aircraft and the accompanying contracts. One of the most profound and drastic examples of this was the armament of the night fighter force. In this instance state-owned businesses such as Junkers or the Messerschmitt AG (privately owned in part) were placed in conflict with the family-owned concerns of Heinkel and Dornier. Instead of rising to the need of the hour and cooperating, these manufacturers zealously plotted against one another. Ernst Heinkel managed to survive with his He 219 "Uhu" design, which may have been able to improve the fatal situation with the night fighters. Unfortunately, however, these examples of poor decision-making, lack of competence, and self-overestimation continued with wholehearted enthusiasm.

A deceptively peaceful scene at a fighter airfield in northern France. The Fw 190A of JG 26 provides a modern contrast to the horse-drawn cart of the French farmer.

The massive B-17 Flying Fortresses of the 8th Air Force have taken off from England and are now heading for Germany. They now carry the war to German soil.

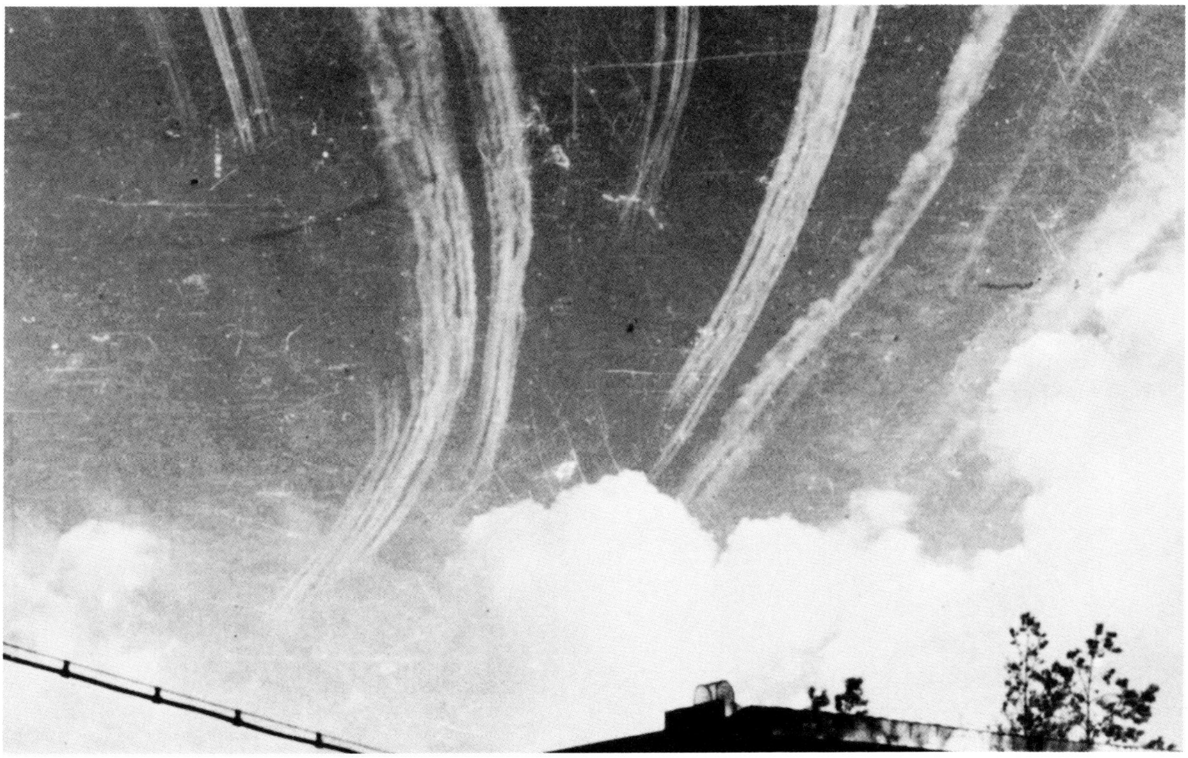

The American bombers have now reached France, and the condensation trails mark the path these war machines of death and destruction are taking.

Scramble for 5/JG 26, the "Rote Fünf" (Red Five). With one final check of the weapons the unit will take off to intercept the bomber stream.

Aircraft warning units monitor the approaching bombers and report their number, altitude, and direction. Wachtmeister (Master of the Watch) Holz of the Luftnachrichtendienst (Air Intelligence) branch writes down a radio message to be passed on to the affected anti-aircraft division.

Which in turn sounds the alarm via radio for the appropriate anti-aircraft battalions responsible for defensive operations.

The flak battery responsible for a given sector receives the report by field telephone, then makes sure the anti-aircraft predictor, which plots the altitude, direction, and speed of the enemy, is updated.

Shortly after this the guns are ready to fire and the crew are in their positions. Cannoneer #2, the sighting cannoneer, has adjusted the gun based on the data from the anti-aircraft predictor. Now they wait for the order to open fire.

Open fire - and now the magic begins for the American crewmembers of these B-24 Liberators. Black puffs of smoke mark the detonations of the 88mm shells.

Maj. Egon Mayer, commander of JG 2 "Richthofen", which, together with JG 26, bore the air defense burden in the West at the beginning of the Allied air offensive.

The vertical stabilizer of Olt. Josef "Sepp" Wurmhellers Fw 190. Olt. Wurmheller commanded 9/JG 2, which was based in Vannes in 1943; he was one of the most successful "four engine specialists."

The Fw 190 A-1 of Olt. Walter Schneider, the captain of 6/JG 26, during the summer of 1942 in northern France.

The Flieger-HJ (Flying Hitler Youth) was a favored source for the training of future flying personnel.

With their training gliders, the youth perfectly mastered the basics of flight. One of the young fliers anticipates taking off in his glider, towed by his comrades with the aid of rubber cords.

With new clothes and in new surroundings these Hitler Youth are now in the Luftwaffe. Even though their primary motivation for Luftwaffe service is flying, they are not spared the military marching drills - something which obviously pleases none of these recruits.

Done! The first long-awaited powered flight with the instructor is just moments away. Since one never quite knows how one of these flights might end, the address and telephone number of the flight school are painted on the rudder of this Bü 131 as a precaution.

This photo shows how necessary this measure was. A Bü 131 has come to rest doing a headstand in a grove of birch trees.

Even students can do such things! On his first solo flight, a student took off from a flight school in the East and plowed directly into a house which bordered on the airfield.

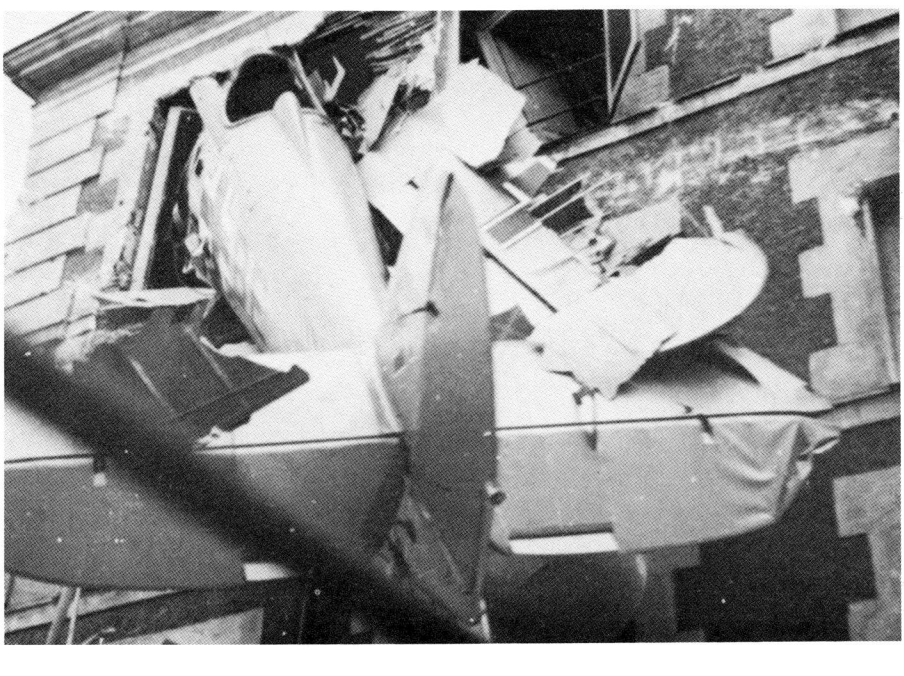

These photos represent the various aircraft used for flight training; from above is the Fw 56 "Stösser" (Hawk), the Ar 68 which was formerly the Luftwaffe's primary fighter until 1938, and the Ar 96B, which was used for specialized fighter pilot training.

And then it was finally over. Here the "freshly baked" pilot Ogfr. Ernst strikes a regal pose for the camera, showing off his pilot's insignia. Now it's straight into the hell of the Reich defense.

Day Fighter Losses 1939-1945	Degree of Damage		
	10-60%	60-100% (complete)	total
through enemy action	6100	16,400	22,500
other	12,900	8600	21,500
	19,000	25,000	44,000

"Zerstörer" and Night Fighter Losses 1939-1945			
through enemy action	1200	3600	4800
other	3100	3100	6200
	4300	6700	11,000

Personnel Losses	Dead	Missing (including prisoners)	Injured
day fighters	8500	2700	9100
"Zerstörer", night fighters	2800	900	1700

A rare photograph of the Do 217 with the code R4+DC. This is the aircraft of Helmut Lent, who flew out of Leeuwarden in 1943 as commander of II/NJG 2. Lent used this aircraft on extremely dark nights. In addition to an auxiliary fuel tank installed in the fuselage, the airplane had a pack holding two 20mm cannons mounted on the lower fuselage in front of the crew hatch. It also carried four machine guns in the upper nose and two machine cannons in the lower nose.

The Kommodore (senior commander) of NJG 1, Wearer of the Oak Leaves to the Knight's Cross Otl. Jabs, together with the leaders under his command, seen in Deelen; from left to right: Maj. Sutor, Maj. Schnaufer, commander of IV/NJG 1, Maj. Drewes, commander of III/NJG 1, Otl. Jabs, commanding officer of NJG 1, Maj. Förster, commander of I/NJG 1, and Maj. von Bonin, commander of II/NJG 1.

A rather involved game of Skat being played by members of JG 3 at the airfield of Shipol near Amsterdam. Those participating are, from left to right: Kloss, Fesshahn, Fröhlich, Kirshner, Brock and Grünberg.

But the hand is quickly over once the alarm sirens scream across the airfield and the pilots of the alert Rotte scramble to their aircraft.

Soon afterwards, the Bf 109 fighters of III/JG 3 "Udet" take off on a new mission.

B-17 bombers seen dropping their deadly cargo. While the American Air Force dropped only 2003 tons of bombs in 1942, this increased to 133089 tons in 1943, 890661 tons in 1944, and 437670 tons in 1945.

"Beating up" the airfield, a successful fighter aircraft returns from a sortie. The airfield's hangars and buildings are well camouflaged against aerial reconnaissance.

The pilot taxis the aircraft to the hangars, where he will turn it around to point toward the taxiway. If needed, this makes it that much easier to get the aircraft back in the air more quickly.

Tired, but obviously pleased with his victory, the pilot raises the heavy canopy with its armored glass and headrest.

This B-17 has the appropriate name of "Rough Wolf"; it has 25 missions behind it, during which the crew has claimed 10 German fighters were shot down.

174 **In the meantime the Messerschmitt fighter is overhauled. The "black men" have their hands full, whether they be engine, radio, or weapons technicians.**

A B-17 is attacked by an Fw 190 while returning from a bombing mission against the Ago Works in Oschersleben. The Ago Works produced the Fw 190 fighters under license. While the fighter, seen behind the bomber on its left, banks to make another attack run, the bomber's inboard port engine is already burning.

Still hurting from his last operational sortie, Lt Benatsch leaves the field clinic. His colleagues, including the Wearer of the Knight's Cross Ofw. Rüffler, are seen discussing the tactics for the next mission.

The "Seeburg Table", named after its inventor, is the plotting board for all information coming into the night fighter direction center. The reports are received from the German "Würzburg-Riese" (Würzburg Giant) radar system. One radar unit has acquired the enemy aircraft, another the friendly fighter. These two plots then appear as red and green blips on the plotting glass of the "Seeburg Table."

The results of the radar plotting are then transmitted to operations center, from which communications are maintained with the individual airborne night fighters. The fighter direction officer directs the fighters to an intercept with the enemy based on the data received from the "Seeburg Table." By reading the board in the background, one can easily check to see which units at which time and from which airfield are currently operating.

A Bf 110 night fighter on its way to its patrol area.

A British Halifax bomber seen during a night bombing raid. Its silhouette, like those of the falling bombs, can clearly be made out above the glow of the burning German city.

The mute witnesses to the bitter air battles of the previous night can be found in the morning, while the search for survivors and the massive cleanup begins in the cities.

A Bf 110 of 7/NJG 1 took hits while attack a bomber, which forced the pilot to make a night emergency landing.

This aircraft was shot down by British long-range night fighters; the crew died in the crash.

A united group: pilot, crew chief, and weapons crewman.

In February of 1944 II/JG 3 was based in Rothenburg near Bremen.

The hunters have now turned into the hunted. Hidden among the trees, concealment has now become the order of the day for the German fighters. Even the maintenance vehicles are not excluded.

The English Mosquito was a dangerous opponent, also used as a bomber. This aircraft bears the black and white markings of the Invasion air armada.

Only when the enemy approaches can the fighter aircraft leave their hiding places and break clear of the forest.

The American bombers, which carried out the daylight bombing campaign, were protected by a strong fighter escort. Two Thunderbolt fighters fly over just above the bombers, while higher up numerous US fighters fly in their intercept positions.

Lost in thought, Lt. Leopold Münster studies the map; in the background is a lineup of Bf 109 G-6 of II/JG 3, ready to take off.

Consolidated B-24 Liberator bombers, along with their North American P-51 Mustang fighter escorts, fly above the North Sea in the direction of northern Germany.

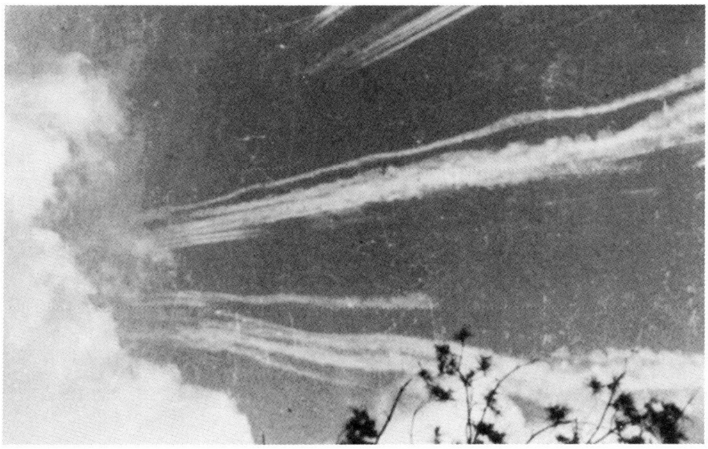

A picture which became all too frequent to German eyes from 1942 on - the condensation trails of an American bomber formation.

Lt. Münster checks the skies one more time before taking off. Where are the enemy fighters and bombers? The Wearer of the Knight's Cross is aware of the dangers of being surprised just as he's taking off.

On the 8th of May, 1944, Lt. Münster was killed while attacking B-24s near Hildesheim. A crater marks the spot where his aircraft struck the ground.

A truck carries the remains of his aircraft's fuselage and wings, while the trailer holds the propeller and parts of the horizontal stabilizer. Lt. Münster was posthumously awarded the Oak Leaves to the Knight's Cross.

The waiting for the next mission orders is passed by making small talk.

It was especially unpleasant to have to sit on alert in the brewing midday heat, but the trick with the umbrella has already gotten around.

And again, its back to attacking against hundreds of Browning machine guns protected by strong armor plates. The German fighters need a boost in their weapons, which is provided by gondolas mounted under the wings.

The American bombers weren't camouflaged. They remained untouched from German bombers or attack aircraft on their bases in England. Over Germany, they were protected by their escort fighters and were perfectly capable of defending themselves with 16 large caliber machine guns. The column of smoke is from a marker bomb, dropped to show the wind's direction.

Wearer of the Oak Leaves to the Knight's Cross Hptm. Kirschner revels with his comrades in the day's victories. The fact that all of them have safely returned is a special cause for celebration.

Waiting for the next sortie kept the pilots on edge. They spent their breaks between missions doing all kinds of things.

An Fw 190 A-3 of II/JG 1 coming to rest.

A Schwarm of 8/JG 26 climbs to attack altitude, which means in a position above the enemy and with the sun at their backs.

Maj. Heinz Bär, left, and Otl. Gustav Rödel, both battle-hardened veteran commanders of the defense of the Reich. At the time the photo was taken, Bär commanded JG 1, and Rödel JG 27.

Fw 190 A-8s of II/JG 300 lined up as if on show at the airfield in Holzkirchen.

One final check before taking off. Trusting is good, checking is even better!

These men of JG 26's air operations have formed up in a rather unmilitary-looking group to celebrate the birthday of Hptm. Leuschel; in the far front is the birthday basket and a bottle of Beaujolais.

DEATH STRUGGLE IN THE SKIES

What began in the winter of 1943/1944 was finished in 1944 and the first five months of 1945. The German armies found themselves retreating on every front. The Luftwaffe was not in a position to stop the waves of Allied bombers, much less regain air superiority. Without the air superiority the Heer could not conduct successful operations. The Jagdwaffe fought a desperate and hopeless struggle against the British and American bombers and fighters.

By the end of 1944, the bomber force had, for all practical purposes, ceased to exist. Their pilots were crosstrained into fighter pilots, a program which was not successful. In addition, the Luftwaffe misplayed its final trump card, the Me 262. This was the first production-built jet bomber in the world. Flown by retrained bomber pilots as a type of "Blitzbomber", it was intended to stop the Allies. This, however, was a totally unviable approach; in the first place, Germany was in dire straits and desperately needed a superior fighter in order to successfully prosecute a defensive air campaign. In the second place, the Me 262 was far to fast to accurately drop its bombs, and in the third place it carried only two 250kg bombs - much to little of a load to make a sortie of any significant impact. And so the last chance was missed to win back the initiative in the air battles which took place in German skies. In the East, Oberst Rudel could still wrest victories from Russian tanks with his "Kanonenvögel" (cannonbirds). In doing so, the Ju 87 celebrated a rather late triumph, a triumph which was possible only on the Eastern Front, where the enemy's fighter defenses were much weaker than those on the Western Front. In the West, such operations by Stukas would have been practically impossible. The successes in the East were fruitless, but they did provide a respite of a few hours or a day for the hard-pressed German ground troops.

The war was lost. The chance for Germany to emerge as victor in the war was also lost, if ever there had even been such a chance. The wings of the eagle - symbol of the Luftwaffe - had been broken.

These Fw 190 A-3s of II/JG 1 are seen at their airfield in northern France. A midday stillness has settled over the well-camouflaged airfield facilities.

Only the armorers are still at work, feeding ammunition belts into the MG 151/20 20mm guns mounted in the wing blisters of an Fw 190.

A formation of ingressing Flying Fortresses; in the foreground can be seen one of their P-47 Thunderbolt escort fighters.

And the bombs fall once again. The German defenses, which were quite effective through 1943, have been crippled. The demands were too great, the expansion of the territory to large to effectively defend. And then there were the fatal miscalculations of Hitler and the Luftwaffe's top leadership.

The German civilian population also had to pay for those errors in judgment. The air war, with which Hitler had threatened Coventry so oppressively, now had come to Germany. These people sitting in the basement of a Koblenz school, and others like them throughout Germany, were not guilty of this war.

Following an air attack, many cities in Germany suffered the same fate as the Münzplatz in Koblenz during March of 1944.

All hands are needed to help with cleaning up. There isn't too much left over anymore.

And again and again, there are the innocent victim such as women, children, and old people. The British came in the night with their carpet bombing; during the day it was the Americans with their point attacks against important military targets.

With four heavy machine guns in each wing, a powerful and reliable engine, and a healthy supply of fuel in the tanks, the Thunderbolt was a worthy opponent of the German fighters.

The pilot of this German fighter aircraft was fortunate, for he was able to bring his injured "Beule" (or bump, referring to all the blisters on later versions of the Bf 109) safely to earth, even if he couldn't use his gear.

The German fighters could have had a great opportunity. US fighters returned from their missions one day with photos of an unusual aircraft missing its propeller. It could overtake or turn circles around its enemies with its superior speed - something its opponents had never thought possible.

They had encountered the first series-produced jet fighter in the world, the Me 262. But it wasn't only its high speed which made it a superior design; it also possessed four machine cannons and a gyroscopic gunsight.

A flak battery seen as twilight falls. The burden of air defense for Germany fell upon the anti-aircraft units more and more - both during the day as well as at night.

The night fighters suffered from the Reich Air Ministry's poor technical decisions and frustrating incompetence just as much as their daytime colleagues.

Maj. Prince zur Lippe-Weissenfeld, a successful night fighter and commander of NJG 5, is seen here paying a visit to a divisional command post.

During the night they're maintaining operational aircraft, in the daytime they're repairing damaged aircraft; even those with the strongest constitution sometimes have to get some shuteye.

In order to provide relief to the bitterly fighting troops of the Heer, Fw 190G fighter-bombers attack Allied supply columns. These were mere pinpricks in comparison to the British and American fighter-bomber operations.

This could happen to an unfortunate front-line vacationer! This train was derailed by US fighter-bombers shortly before reaching the homeland.

Col. Thomas Christian of the 375th Fighter Squadron in his North American P-51D Mustang, photographed during the Invasion. This aircraft was a successful design of the American aircraft manufacturers.

The last, futile battle of a Bf 109 against a superior foe. This photo was taken from the automatic gun camera of Lt. Leroy W. Ista's Mustang.

In Löbnitz Fw. Hubert Engst climbs into the cockpit of his "yellow 2", an Fw 190 A-8 of JG 301.

After the throat microphone is adjusted and the bulletproof glass canopy is closed, there follows a brief moment of concentration on the terrible hours that lie ahead for him. Directly in front of his face can be seen the reflexive gunsight.

And what possibilities could the German fighters have had! Much too late, and even then in limited numbers, the Me 262 - the most modern andcombat-capable aircraft in the world - reached only a few test units. This one is seen at the Nowotny test unit in Achmer.

Otl. Hannes Trautloft, inspector of the day fighters, wears a skeptical expression as he leaves a two-seat Me 262B-1 following a test flight. He is conscious of the fact that the aircraft is too late in coming.

The fighter pilot aces have come together once more in Genlt. Galland's JV 44. The "white 13" was flown by Maj. Bär from Lechfeld.

An Me 262 is seen taking off. Having been hitherto degraded from the hunter to the hunted, the German fighter pilot was once again given a taste of absolute superiority.

Both Maj. Barkhorn (above) and Hptm. Krupinski (below) were members of JV 44.

Hitler's senseless fixation with the idea of making the Me 262 into a type of "Blitzbomber" caused delays of more than a year in the delivery of the turbo-fighter to front-line units. Even then, only a small percentage of the 1500 aircraft which were built made it to the fighter units. Even with the Me 262 the war would have been lost, but tens of thousands of bombing victims would still be alive today.

Once again, an aircraft from the Nowotny test unit. The aircraft of this unit can be recognized by their brightly colored rudders.

"Pimpf" (wolf cub) Mattäus Erhard. The average age of replacement fighter pilots had dropped rapidly and, unfortunately, so did their level of training. Many didn't survive their first sortie.

Those that were fortunate came under the protection and experience of a wise old hand, as Gfr. Erhard has found in Uffz. Schröder. The Fw 190 A-8 is Erhard's aircraft, and with little difficulty the nickname "Pimpf" can be seen beneath the cockpit canopy.

210 Again and again, German fighters such as these powerhouses of JG 300 emerge from forests and hedges to fight against an overpowering foe.

A dangerous landing following a tough sortie. If the fighters were fortunate enough to survive the hell of the air battle, they still had several dangerous minutes ahead of them during their landings. It was at this phase of relative helplessness that American fighters, which had been circling the airfields and waiting for the returning German fighters, often chose to pounce.

By this time the German bomber units had, for all practical purposes, ceased to exist. The pilots were retrained as fighter or fighter-bomber pilots, which succeeded only in the rarest of cases. Only a few units continued to operate, carrying out special missions. This He 111 H-6 of KG 26 is performing one of these special missions, delivering a 1800kg bomb to a bridge. There were, however, plenty of bombs, as this photo shows.

Otl. Rudel operated with greater efficiency using his "Kanonenvögel." Carrying two 37mm anti-tank guns under its wings, the Ju 87 G-1 enjoyed outstanding success on the Eastern Front. Rudel himself destroyed 518 Russian tanks from the air. That is equivalent to more than five Russian tank corps.

Each morning, the pilots of JG 300 leave their quarters in Löbnitz bound for the airfield on the city's outskirts - a November day in 1944.

The pilots crowd into the command post to receive their daily briefing. No one is certain who will be there the following day.

Wearer of the Knight's Cross Lt. Bretschneider, sitting to the far left, assigns the pilots to their "Schwärme" for the day. As the war progresses, it becomes more and more difficult to pair the young and inexperienced pilots with the "old hands", and giving them a chance to survive the day's combat.

The Allied fighters and fighter-bombers are now to be seen everywhere. Hardly a street or bridge hasn't been cratered with the bombs and guns of the fighter-bombers.

For a long time now, the German fighters have found themselves in the role of the hunted. An Fw 190 is taking hits; chunks of the fuselage can be seen falling away.

All that the senior leader of the Luftwaffe has to offer his commanders and troops during the fateful final months of the war are great and empty gestures.

General of the Fighters, Genlt. Galland, together with his Geschwader leaders, desperately attempts to avoid the worst - but without success. The man standing is the Jagdführer (Leader of the Fighters) for Italy, Wearer of the Swords to the Knight's Cross Otl. Lützow. Due to his outspoken criticism, he experienced the wrath of Göring and was punished with a Reichsverbot, whereby he was stripped of many of his rights as a citizen in the Reich. He fell in air-to-air combat during the final weeks of the war.

General der Flieger (General of the Fighters) Adolf Galland and his successor, Otl. Gordon Gollob. The two officers, both awarded the Diamonds to the Knight's Cross, didn't care much for one another.

This photograph is a chronicle which testifies as to how drastic the situation had become for the fighter pilots during the last phase of the Reich defense; left to right: Uffz. Werner, fallen on 02 March 1945, Uffz. Schröder, who provided this photo, was shot down several times but somehow managed to survive, Ofw. Winter, killed on 17 December 1944, Ofw. Piel, killed on 29 November 1944, Olt. Maier from gunnery school, Lt. Graziadei, killed in action, Ofhr. Schneider, killed on 27 November 1944, Fj. Ofw. Löfgren, fallen on 02 March 1945. With the exception of Ofw. Winter, who was from 6 Staffel, all were members of 5/JG 300.

Nothing would have been possible without them, the men in their black overalls, the engine mechanics and weapons loaders, the landing gear and airframe specialists, the radio mechanics and bomb loaders. Upon them rested the blind faith of the flying crews. Without receiving the awards and decorations, without being mentioned in the Wehrmacht reports, they nevertheless played a major role in the victories of men such as Mölders, Marseille, Baumbach, Peltz, Rudel, Druschel, and all the others.

US escort fighters were now operating from bases near the Reich borders, some even from German soil. A P-51D returns from a mission to land, while in the background a liaison aircraft prepares to take off.

A Mustang is parked in front of the remains of a burned-out German aircraft. American fighters are still guarded by soldiers, since there is yet the possibility of attacks or acts of sabotage.

Fewer and fewer aircraft are able to take off from those airfields still remaining in German hands. This is a Ju 88 C-4 of II/NJG 2, heading out on one of its nighttime missions.

Cow mockups placed on the runway are designed to fool the prying eyes of enemy reconnaissance aircraft.

But it didn't help much and certainly not for long; the bombers always seemed to find the airfields.

All that was left were bombed-out airfields and burned-out airplane hulks, and the concern over having to find an alternate place to operate from.

The metal nose of a Ju 88 night fighter has been removed, leaving bare the barrels of the machine cannons in front of the armored plating.

The mechanics of 3/NJG 2 seen here during a break. This photo was taken at an airfield in Holland in 1943; notice that the aircraft are still kept parked in the open.

In 1944/1945, this is the way things looked. This is an example of a bomber unit in Schleissheim near Munich.

Still half children, these youth have matured through the horror of the bombing campaign. This is a class of students being trained in a Koblenz public high school to provide assistance to the anti-aircraft units of the Flugabwehr.

A flak position is readied for the nightly battle. The guns and searchlights are being adjusted.

And then it's time! Shell after shell roars from the barrel of the gun, which can be seen clearly against the bright background of the muzzle flash.

A hit - an English bomber has been damaged by a near miss and the right wing is already burning as a new shell explodes next to the cockpit. The glowing shell fragments can be seen leaving a burning trail. The ground is illuminated as bright as day thanks to the parachute flares, also called Christmas trees, drifting slowly to earth.

Ofw. Richter in his powerwagon. This Fw 190 A-8 was reinforced by additional armor plating on the cockpit sides and strengthened bulletproof glass on the canopy's front and sides. This armor plating was designed to protect the pilot from the murderous defensive fire he had to brave in order to get close enough to the bombers to score a killing shot.

In spite of all the extra protection. This photo documents the funeral of Uffz. Werner on 21 July 1944 in Löbnitz.

And so it continues. Again and again, the German fighters return to combat, even when there are forty American aircraft flying for every German aircraft.

Refueling, rearming, and patching up the damage - and then back in the air again. In between, the pilot has little time to catch some sleep.

With two WG 21 rocket tubes under each wing and additional heavy caliber armament under the fuselage, the Bf 110 "Zerstörer" has also been thrown into the fray of the Reich defense. An act of pure desperation.

This "Zerstörer" was hounded by the American bombers' escort fighters and seriously damaged. The pilot was still able to crashland his aircraft in a field near Trier.

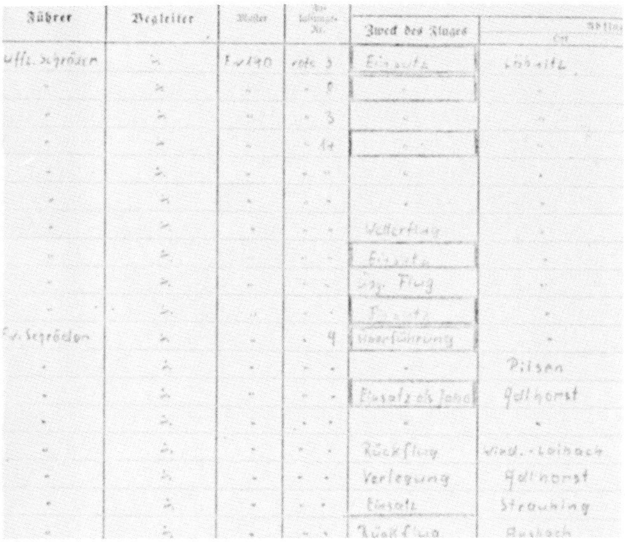

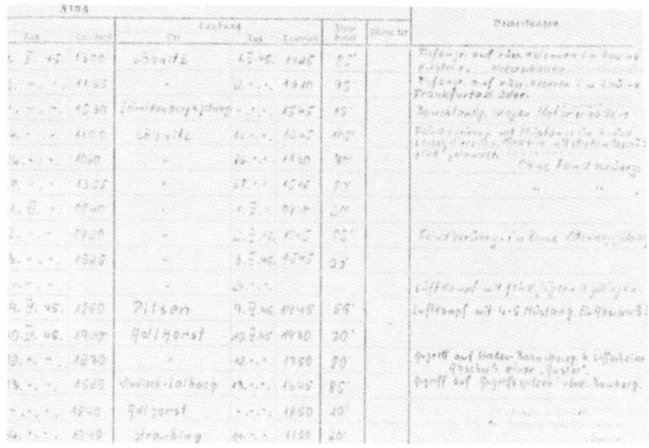

A page from Fw. Schröder's logbook documents a few weeks during the Reich defense: from the northeast to the north, from the far west to the east and from there to the south, and being shot or forced down several times. This was the day-to-day life for a pilot in the German Luftwaffe during those days.

Takeoff into uncertainty. As he takes off, the pilot isn't sure where he'll be able to land or, more importantly, how he'll be coming back to earth.

This pilot it returning by way of parachute. After being shot at by US fighters, this pilot has bailed out of his Bf 109 and falls toward earth.

The Fw fighters were outstanding machines and superior to the Bf 109 in many respects. But even they aren't capable of dealing with the Mustang threat.

A superior replacement was the Fw 190 D-9, which proved itself to be on par with, if not superior to, its American opponents. But again, it was the same old story: ". . . too little and too late!"

An Fw 190 D-9 has attacked a USAAF 8th Air Force B-26 formation and dives away below the Marauders. In doing so, it almost gets caught in the cluster of falling bombs.

Perhaps even more so than the carpet bombing of the massive US bomber formations, the American fighter-bombers contributed to the total collapse of the German resupply effort. No street or railroad was safe from their bombs and eight guns, seen here to good advantage.

Even the Luftwaffe was caught by the fighter-bombers; using its guns, an English Tempest destroyed this Ta 152 of Hq JG 301 in Hannover-Langenhagen, 1945.

The German fighter pilots never lost their humor and unbridled lust for life.

A mock cow provides a cozy resting place; it has outlived its usefulness since the enemy is no longer fooled by such methods.

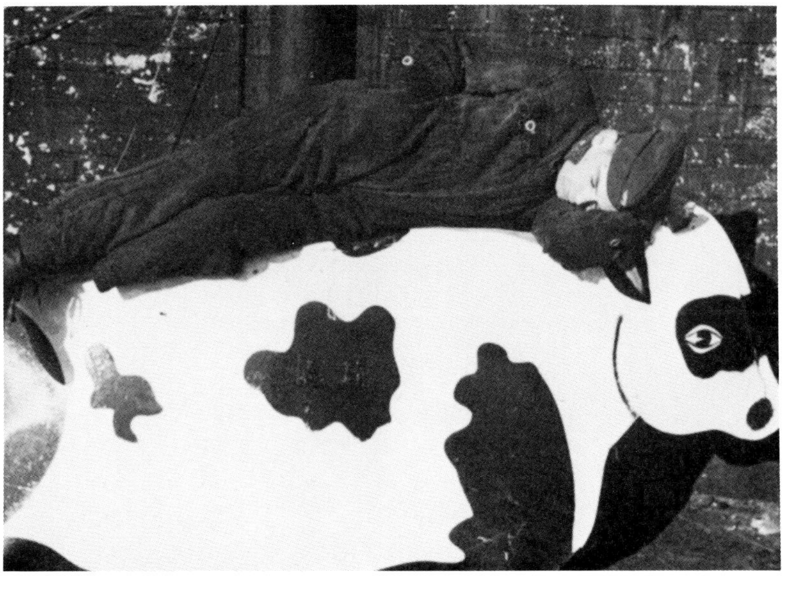

A last stand by the Luftwaffe, primarily its fighters, was more than just a desperate measure. What was intended by the Luftwaffe's leadership as a massive strike against enemy airfields turned into the Jagdwaffe's darkest day - Operation "Bodenplatte." Fw. Werner Hohenberg, of I/JG 26, crashlanded his Fw 190 D-9 on January 1st, 1945, near Lüttich. Like this aircraft, more than a third of all the participating German aircraft were either shot down or heavily damaged. The German anti-aircraft units played a particularly inglorious role by shooting down a number of their own aircraft. They hadn't been informed of the operation, but should have known they were friendlies by the aircrafts' flight direction and by proper recognition of the low flying fighters.

The train station at the Alt-Lönnewitz airfield. The train was supposed to bring in Ar 234 parts for final assembly, but these, the first twin engine jet bombers in the world were never delivered - May, 1945.

Another "wonder weapon", the He 162, was never flown in combat. They were built deep in mines in the Harz Mountains and were planned as a relief for the hard pressed day fighters. These He 162 Salamanders of JG 1 in Leck/Holstein were never used operationally and were handed over to the English near the end of the war.

Germany's only strategic bomber, the He 177, never freed itself from its design flaws. The concept of coupling two engines one behind the other caused fires again and again, a feature which gave the aircraft its nickname of "the Reich's cigarette lighter" or "the Reich's torch."

An interesting detail photo of the cockpit nose. Aside from the pivoting MG 81 machine guns, the aircraft also carried a fixed machine cannon mounted in a tray beneath the canopy.

The entire fleet of He 177s was transferred to Norway at the end of 1944, where they participated in actions against Allied convoys bound for Murmansk. Wearer of the Oak Leaves to the Knight's Cross Bernhard Jope was the commander of this unit.

An Fw 190 D-9 of II/JG 301 in Stendal in February of 1945. The aircraft of this Gruppe used their internal guns and bombs to carry out the war in the East, which by then had moved onto German soil.

An Fw 190 D-9 taking off with a 250kg bomb slung beneath its belly.

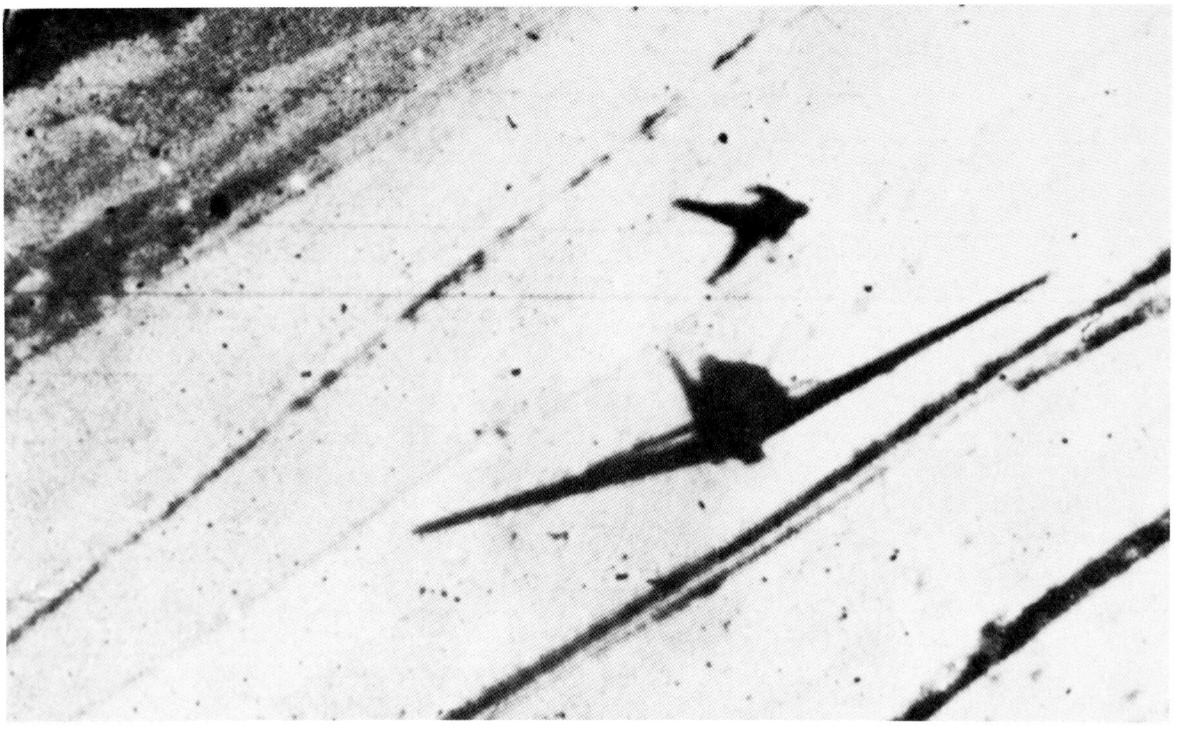

Bailout - the last avenue left for a young, inexperienced, and poorly trained pilot to avoid an otherwise certain death during the defense of the Reich.

The center of Koblenz following a devastating bombing attack in February 1945. This photo was taken by a low flying American Lightning reconnaissance aircraft. Koblenz was attacked primarily because it was the crossroads of strategically important routes to the West.

Uffz. Beuchel ploughed into a parked Fw 190 during takeoff. He escaped with a good scare and a burned face.

Humor, even bitter humor, is when one can still enjoy a good laugh in spite of everything. Fw. Schröder obviously kept his native Cologne humor about him, something which allowed him to take many things a bit more lightheartedly. ("Kölle alaaf" is a toast often heard at Cologne's famous Carnival festivities).

The game is up! Without fuel or pilots, hunted from airfield to airfield, the last proud representative of the Luftwaffe, the Jagdwaffe, is finished. A false sense of priorities and a blind adherence to Hitler's rigid offensive doctrine led to a rapid demise.

They and their companions in the other flying units had given their best, and in many cases paid the highest price - their lives. Uffz. Schröder's Schwarm: from left to right is Uffz. Schröder, Ofw. Richter, killed on 24 March 1945, Uffz. Straub, missing in action, and Uffz. Bastek, also killed on 24 March 1945.

The war is over. A Thunderbolt makes a low level pass over Hitler's Berghof near Berchtesgaden, which has been completely destroyed by an American bombing attack. This photograph symbolizes the victory of the American Air Force over the German Wehrmacht.

APPENDIX: Translator's Note

As the reader will have noticed, Luftwaffe units have been referred to in the text using their original German terms. Most German Luftwaffe units had no direct counterpart in the RAF or USAAF, thereby making an accurate translation rather difficult. The basic unit in the Jagdwaffe was the Rotte, consisting of a wing leader and his wingman. A formation of three aircraft, called a Kette, was also flown quite often. Two Rotten comprised a Schwarm, and approximately three Schwärme made up a Staffel (for a rough total ranging from nine to sixteen aircraft). Three or four Staffeln formed a Gruppe, and three or four Gruppen made up a Geschwader. A Geschwader, therefore, could conceivably embrace anywhere from just over 80 aicraft to nearly 200 aircraft. A unit's strength also depended on the time period in question; as the war progressed, the number of aircraft in many a unit would often dropped considerably, sometimes taking weeks or even months to be brought back up to strength. By the end of the war, many Gruppen were operating with only a handful of operationally capable aircraft. In the text, Staffeln are indicated by Arabic numerals, subordinated to their corresponding Geschwader, e.g. 2/JG 3. Gruppen are likewise subordinated to their Geschwader, but are indicated by Roman numerals, such as IV/ZG 76. The reason Staffeln are subordinated to Geschwader instead of to their Gruppen is a logical one: the Staffel number indicates to which Gruppe it is subordinate. 1, 2, and 3 Staffel are subordinate to I Gruppe, 4, 5, and 6 Staffel to II Gruppe, 7, 8, and 9 Staffel to III Gruppe, and 10, 11, and 12 Staffel to IV Gruppe. Thus, 2/JG 3 would indicate 2 Staffel, I Gruppe, Jagdgeschwader 3. An explanation of the unit abbreviations used in this book follows.

Abbreviation	Explanation
E/JG	Jagdgeschwaderergänzungsgruppe, or Replacement Training Gruppe of a Fighter Geschwader
JG	= Jagdgeschwader, or Fighter Geschwader
KG	= Kampfgeschwader, or Bomber Geschwader
Kü.Fl.Gr	= Küstenfliegergruppe, or Coastal Patrol Gruppe
LG	= Lehrgeschwader, or Training Geschwader
NJG	= Nachtjagdgeschwader, or Night Fighter Geschwader
StG	= Sturzkampfgeschwader, or Stuka Geschwader
ZG	= Zerstörergeschwader, or Bf 110 (Destroyer) Geschwader

Individual ranks have also been left untranslated and abbreviated as they appeared in the original German text. The following is a listing of German Luftwaffe rank abbreviations found in this book.

Fw.	Feldwebel	Maj.	Major
Gef.	Gefreiter	Ofhr.	Oberfähnrich
Gen.	General	Ofw.	Oberfeldwebel
Genlt.	Generalleutnant	Ogfr.	Obergefreiter
Gfm	Generalfeldmarschall	Olt.	Oberleutnant
Hptm.	Hauptmann	Otl.	Oberstleutnant
Ltn.	Leutnant	Uffz.	Unteroffizier

Many of the pilots mentioned in the pages of this book have been noted as receiving the Ritterkreuz, or Knight's Cross. It was the highest honor a German officer could receive during World War II, and was actually an extension of another famous German award - Das Eiserne Kreuz, or the Iron Cross. It is therefore sometimes mentioned as the Knight's Cross of the Iron Cross and was only awarded to those who had previously received the Iron Cross. In addition to the Knight's Cross itself, an officer could be awarded additional adornments to the award: Oak Leaves to the Knight's Cross (Eichenlaub), Swords to the Knight's Cross (Schwerter), and the highest, Diamonds to the Knight's Cross (Brillanten).

German Military Rifles and Machine Pistols 1871-1945

Hans Dieter Götz

This richly illustrated volume portrays the development of the modern German weapons and their ammunition, and includes many rare and experimental types. Among the weapons covered in this book are the Werder rifle, Mauser rifles, the various M/71 rifles and ammunition, the 88 cartridge, the infantry rifle 88, ther 98 rifles, the 41 & 43 rifles, the Fallschirmjäger rifle, ERMA & Walther assault rifles, the STEN copy and many more. Value guide included.

Size: 8 1/2" x 11"   248 pp.
Many documents, line drawings, over 200 photos
ISBN: 0-88740-264-X   hard cover $35.00

The German Infantry Handbook 1939-1945

Alex Buchner

Many millions of soldiers belonged to the more than 500 German infantry divisions between 1939-1945. But was an infantry division like at that time? What sort of form did it take, and how did the structures, the organization, and the equipment of an infantry division look during World War II?

Alex Buchner sets out to give answers to these questions, presenting the first inclusive picture of the German infantry. It illuminates the inner connections and describes everything that made up an infantry division at that time – formation, strength, armament, equipment, rank insignias, rifle groups, rifle columns, the company, light infantry weapons, reconnaissance units, Panzerjäger units, the artillery regiment, engineer battalions, veterinary services, information units, support services, medical services, new infantry weapons, divisional casualties and much more. This is an important work of war history, unfolding a hitherto unseen portrait in text and pictures.

For historians and for those interested in the history of men at war, this volume will become one of the classics in the literature on the German Wehrmacht.

Size: 7" x 10" over 225 photos 288pp.

ISBN: 0-88740-284-4 hard cover $29.95

First English Edition

Paul Carell's

OPERATION BARBAROSSA IN PHOTOGRAPHS

The War in Russia as Photographed by the Soldiers

se photos are irreplaceable witnesses of the war in the east, and impressively and inclusively illustrate what Carell ribed so grippingly in words in his superb Russian Front studies, *Hitler Moves East*, and *Scorched Earth*. in his textual volumes, Carell not only utilizes the German sources in this photo volume, but also those of the one enemy: the photo archives of the Russians. With the support of the Soviet embassy and the Novosti Agency, more four hundred documentary photos could be obtained from the Soviet Union and evaluated. They show what no cameraman saw: the other side of the war. This volume of photographs is a genuine Carell work — objective, ripping.

0" 458 pp. Over 570 b/w & color photographs, charts, maps, insignia and divisionsal listings
40-280-1 hard cover $44.95

The
des
As
time
than
Germa
factual, g
Size: 7" x
ISBN: 0-88